Doctor
Deals

Doctor Deals

Nicholas A. Newsad, MHSA

With Kyle D. Tormoehlen, ASA, MBA

ISBN 13: 978-0-9828039-4-3
ISBN 10: 0-9828039-4-X
LCCN: 2014943553

Edited by Bonnie Granat
Cover Photo: © iStock, Mark Wragg.
Cover Design by Allan P. Ytac
Typeset by Colleen Rollins

Printed in the United States of America

Table of Contents

INTRODUCTION

This is a tactical playbook for anyone who wants to be successful in the business of fighting disease. This book distills the observations that my business partner Kyle Tormoehlen and I have made during our involvement in over 600 business deals between physicians, hospitals, and other types of healthcare organizations. They don't teach this stuff in medical school, business school, or law school. We have created a catalogue of the state of the art of healthcare deal making.

The division of expertise in the realm of healthcare between physicians, healthcare executives, and attorneys is like having three people all playing on one side of a chess match. One team member is in charge of physically moving the pieces, one is in charge of keeping track of all the pieces, and one is in charge of knowing the rules.

In healthcare, physicians are the only members of the team who are allowed to actually practice medicine, healthcare executives are responsible for the major financial resources and investments, and attorneys are responsible for knowing all the laws and advising physicians and healthcare executives on what we can and cannot do. With this awkward triad, it's not difficult to understand why it is so hard just to get the day-to-day work done. In this environment, it takes real guts to stick your neck out for a special project that will likely either get shot down for technical reasons outside your area of expertise or fall victim to a slow, painful death-by-meetings.

When used properly, good tactics make normal people seem much smarter than they actually are because they can get better results than peers with access to the exact same resources. Chess players all start the game with the same pieces, but with time, good tactics can promote even a tiny pawn into a powerful queen. Good opening gambits, forks, sacrifices, decoys, combinations, and material investments are just as valid in business as they are in chess.

However, recently great tactical execution has been losing the popularity contest to a wave of *strategic initiatives* and *strategic thinking*. *Strategy* is probably the most incorrectly used buzzword in all of business. *Strategies* are relatively simple, long-term plans that generally guide how businesses will achieve their goals. According to management guru Michael Porter, there are really only three types of strategies. They are low-cost leadership, product differentiation, and focused market segmentation. I might add *monopoly* as a fourth strategy that applies in healthcare.

Strategies are overarching, long plays that are set in stone for 10 years or so. Once these philosophical ways of doing business are set, they are not very susceptible to change.

However, there are an infinite number of *tactics* for achieving your strategic goals. Tactics are all the novel little tricks and *moves* that you learn during a long career of playing the game. Tactical decisions are where 99% of the real action is.

Carl von Clausewitz put it another way, "Tactics is the art of using troops in battle; strategy is the art of using battles to win the war."

It is really the CEOs' responsibility to decide *what* strategy to pursue and *why*. It is everyone else's job to figure out *how* to make it happen.

Dwight D. Eisenhower ultimately rose from being a brigadier general to become the supreme commander of all Allied Forces during World War II because he proved to General George C. Marshall that he was adept at converting broad strategies into great tactical battle plans. Eisenhower was very effective at turning concepts and ideas into practical actions.

This book identifies the commonly used business tactics that are holding together the American healthcare system and explains *why* these linchpins are more critical than ever. The title of this book, *Doctor Deals*, refers to these tactics; they are monumentally important yet often misunderstood or esoteric to all but the most seasoned healthcare business professionals.

Garry Kasparov was the world chess champion for fifteen years from 1985 to the year 2000, and is perhaps the greatest chess player of all time. Kasparov advises students to not only memorize the classic plays by great chess players of the past but to also know why they made every move. According to Kasparov, memorization is equivalent to working from a cookbook. Creativity is knowing every recipe in the cookbook and crafting a new one.

You can learn to master healthcare business tactics the same way you learn to master chess. But you don't have to memorize every move in this book. You merely need to understand when and why to use each tactic.

These tools will be useful to readers' measuring of success in different ways. Different tactics are applicable for different goals. Your goal may be to grow your practice, serve the poor, make more money, improve service quality, improve your quality of life, save lives, defend yourself from a competitor, reduce hospital readmissions, or minimize per member per month medical costs.

Chapter 1 and Chapter 2 are organized to give the reader some historical perspective and practical background on the American medical profession. Some of the information in these chapters may seem elementary to those who have worked in the industry for some time.

Chapter 3 and Chapter 4 catalogue the various types of tactics used in the industry to align physicians and hospitals. Chapter 5 discusses the wave of physician employment deals that have occurred during the past six years.

Chapter 6 contextualizes *Doctor Deals* in terms of other industries and also discusses new changes in the healthcare industry.

Chapter 7 highlights the big problems in our industry and provides some direction for how the tactics presented in this book can be adapted and applied to solve them.

PART I:
DOCTOR DEALS

Chapter 1
The Great Game of Healthcare

OVERVIEW

This chapter discusses the following topics related to the business aspects of the healthcare industry in the United States:

- What Money Can and Cannot Buy in the Healthcare Industry

- Physician Independence and the Ban on the Corporate Practice of Medicine

- Hospitals' Difficulty in Aligning with Physicians

- Vulnerabilities of Individual Physicians as Small Business Owners

The true nature of the healthcare game is a far more fascinating story than any conspiracy theory I could fabricate. It is also too complicated to be summarized in a punchy three-second sound bite for a cable talk show or news segment.

A venture capitalist once told me that if I couldn't describe a healthcare business opportunity in a single sentence, then I wasn't explaining it very well.

In my head I retorted, "You don't know what you're talking about! If it could be explained in one sentence, anyone could do this. It's a great opportunity because it *is* complicated and almost nobody understands it well enough to pursue it. That's the benefit of working in a technical industry."

In the game of chess there are 64 squares on the chessboard, and each player has 16 pieces. The rules for all legal moves can be learned in a day, yet the incredible complexity of the game has occupied men and women for hundreds of years and will continue to do so for many more.

At any given time in the aptly named *middle game* of chess, there are approximately 40 legal moves a player can make, 40 legal responses, and another 40 additional responses. If you attempted to identify all your possible moves and all your opponent's possible responses for just the next four moves that you could make, you would have to calculate over 6.5 trillion scenarios. That is 40 possible moves raised to the power of eight (40^8). This complexity is apparent with a finite number of just 32 pieces and relatively small game board of just 64 squares.

Now imagine being an executive at a health system with over 1,000 employees and 200 privileged physicians. The battlefield is a three-county area with over 1,500 square miles of geography and over a million residents. You are no longer looking at a chessboard but at a map that is alive, moving, and constantly changing right in front of your eyes.

Welcome to the great game of healthcare.

WHAT MONEY CAN AND CANNOT BUY IN THE HEALTHCARE INDUSTRY

In 2004, I read *Buffetology*, a book by Mary Buffet. Her analysis of billionaire Warren Buffet's investment strategies did not make a very strong impression on me at the time, but her description of the intangible characteristics of successful companies lingered in the recesses of my mind during the past 10 years. She said Buffet's ideal company was one that you could not duplicate or compete with even if you had a billion dollars (which Warren Buffet has) and your choice of any management or leadership team in the world (which Warren Buffet could get). She said Buffet preferred to own companies with substantial intangible values that gave those companies a superior competitive advantage that couldn't be duplicated, regardless of how much money was spent on it.

Her example was The Coca-Cola Company. Even if you devoted billions and billions of dollars to developing a new company to compete with Coca-Cola, and you somehow got Jack Welch, Lee Iacocca, and Mark Zuckerberg together to run it, there is still a pretty good probability that you're going to fail miserably and not even make a dent in Coca-Cola's market share. Coca-Cola has got something you just can't duplicate.

This idea stuck with me. There are challenges you simply can't overcome just by throwing extreme amounts of money at them. Some things you can't buy. Some things just aren't for sale.

For the better part of the last decade I have labored as a hospital consultant for close to a hundred different hospitals and health systems. I have often wondered whether I could compete with some of these prestigious medical institutions if I had a billion dollars and my choice of leadership teams.

A billion dollars could absolutely build first-class medical facilities, purchase x-ray machines, MRIs, and CT scanners, and could fund the payment of the thousands of nurses and allied health professionals needed to provide patient care.

But what could money *not* buy?

To the lay person, it would be appear to be extremely difficult—if not impossible—for me to procure the services of the world-class physicians I would need to compete with institutions like The John Hopkins Hospital, Massachusetts General Hospital, MD Anderson Cancer Center, the Mayo Clinic, or the Cleveland Clinic. After all, physicians are independent practitioners, and you can't just throw money at them to get what you want.

In fact, the United States has stiff state and federal laws against paying physicians for patient referrals, and rightly so. Patients' health and well-being is sacred. Physicians can't be coerced to make decisions about patient care based on financial incentives or disincentives. Accordingly, bribing a physician for patient referrals is a violation of the federal Anti-Kickback Statute and is a criminal offence punishable by five years in prison for each occurrence.

So regardless of how much money I have, I can't tell physicians how to treat their patients or where to treat them. Physicians are trained, licensed, and regulated by other physicians. Only physicians are qualified and legally allowed to practice medicine. Only physicians are legally permitted to deliver medical services such as prescribing medications and narcotics, performing surgery, ordering medically necessary diagnostic tests, and interpreting test results.

This reality is a huge problem if I want to invest a billion dollars in a new hospital that will compete with The John Hopkins Hospital. I would be completely reliant on physicians to provide services at my facility, but I couldn't do anything financially to influence their behavior.

On the surface, this seems just like the kind of problem that you can't fix by throwing money at it—or is it?

During the last decade my business partner Kyle and I have been advisors to over 600 doctor deals around the United States, including hundreds of physician–hospital joint venture surgery centers, imaging centers, and surgical and acute-care hospitals. We have done the same for hundreds of contractual doctors deals, including physician employment compensation arrangements, clinical coverage arrangements, and management arrangements.

While I was initially disappointed to find myself being pigeon-hold as a "career consultant," it has become apparent that being designated as such has given me a fantastic perspective that I could have never gained had I taken a management job at a single hospital or physician group. Across the healthcare industry, job roles are inherently very specialized, just as physicians and medical disciplines are very specialized. If I had limited myself to a management position at one hospital, my experiences with physician–hospital relationships would have been limited to the activities of that particular organization. Working for national firms, specializing in all aspects of "physician alignment," as we call it, I have had the great fortune within just a few years to play a role in nearly every type of legal, business, and financial arrangement that exists between physicians and hospitals. I could have spent an entire 40 year career at a single hospital and not seen as many deals as I have working on a national level.

Otto Von Bismarck said, "Fools say that they learn by experience. I prefer to profit by others' experience."

Based on what I have seen and learned, I now believe that anyone with the know-how and the financial means could duplicate the services provided by most U.S. hospitals and health systems. In fact, if they had the know-how, and the financial means, I think that many large employers, cities, counties, states, and small countries could develop fully integrated health systems to meet the entire health needs of their populations.

This book reverse-engineers the tactics that most U.S. hospitals use to provide fundamental medical services, even though physicians are the ones with the medical licenses. It reveals the symbiotic nature of the relationships of physicians and hospitals. It also explores the methods used to "align" physicians with hospitals and health organizations and the slippery slope of compromising physicians' independence.

Aligning physicians with hospitals, while maintaining their independence, is a unique feature of the U.S. healthcare model. Our country's economic system is based on capitalism. While there is a fair amount of regulation, the millions of healthcare providers in the United States primarily operate independently of the government. They freely practice and provide their services autonomously to the public.

PHYSICIAN INDEPENDENCE AND THE BAN ON THE CORPORATE PRACTICE OF MEDICINE

The hospital business is more complicated than most people realize. A unique distinction in American healthcare is that physicians have historically practiced as independent contractors, not employees of hospitals. While there has definitely been a strong shift toward employment of primary care physicians during the last several years, physician independence prevails and continues to make the hospital business complex and difficult to manage.

Approximately half of the states of the United States have made it unlawful for practicing physicians to be employees of corporations. This ban on the "corporate practice of medicine" (CPM) is intended to keep medical professionals independent and free from financial pressures and influence. Many fear that corporate medicine would be bad for patients because the financial pressure that employers may exert on physicians could negatively affect patient care. Most states have made exceptions allowing physicians to become employees of not-for-profit organizations and sometimes hospitals. However, some states, such as California, have applied extremely strict interpretations of the CPM doctrine to make sure physicians always act in the best interest of their patients.

In any case, hospitals cannot make physicians refer patients to their facilities, regardless of whether the physician is independent or employed. Physicians have licenses to practice medicine and make medical decisions in the best interest of their patients. There is nothing that a hospital or anyone else can do to make a physician do anything. Physicians can admit patients to any hospital they want, with no need to explain themselves or defend their decision.

Hospitals do not have medical licenses. Hospital administrators are essentially business people, not medical practitioners. Hospitals provide facilities, equipment, and staff to support physicians' practice of medicine. Only physicians can authorize the medical necessity of services like surgery, medical imaging, pathological testing, and the prescription of narcotics and other controlled substances.

Most states have legislation affirming the commonly held belief that physicians working in a clinical capacity should not be employees of corporations or laypeople. As such, in most states, physicians can only be employed by other physicians, not-for-profit hospitals, or not-for-profit organizations.

These CPM laws have been tested and changed frequently during the past few years. With growing demand for physician services from the aging population and decreased payments from insurance companies, more and more physicians are abandoning their private practices for employment arrangements with large physician groups like Kaiser and hospital-affiliated physician groups.

The laws and exceptions also vary widely from state to state. States such as California, Iowa, and Texas, have declined to allow hospitals to employ physicians, although even those states have special exceptions. Iowa hospitals may employ pathologists and radiologists, and Texas public hospitals and California teaching hospitals may employ physicians.[1] Ohio has no ban on the corporate practice of medicine. Anyone can own a physician practice in Ohio.

HOSPITALS' DIFFICULTY IN ALIGNING WITH PHYSICIANS

Primary care physicians led the shift to hospital employment, and that appears to be driving more specialists to hospital employment as well. Primary care physicians are, after all, the main referral source for specialists. When the primary care physicians are employed by large organizations that also employ specialists like cardiologists and OBGYNs, the primary care physicians tend to refer to specialists within their organization. This is bad for independent specialists because their patient referrals can dry up when the primary care physicians in their communities give up their practices and join a hospital-affiliated group.

I met an orthopedic surgeon in Oregon who described how this happened to him. He noticed very quickly that he had almost no new patients, and his practice was slowing down significantly. He promptly called all of the family practice and internal medicine physicians employed by the local hospital to find out what was going on. He learned that there was a rumor circulating that he was no longer performing surgery at the hospital that employed them and that he was taking his patients elsewhere. As a result, the primary care physicians were referring their patients to other local orthopedic surgeons instead of him. After he explained that the rumor was false, all of his referrals returned.

Strictly speaking, a hospital cannot specifically instruct its employed primary care physicians to refer patients to specific specialists, nor can it prohibit primary care physicians from referring or admitting patients to competing medical facilities. Physicians, even employed physicians, are still independent. No hospital administrator or executive can tell a physician how to practice medicine, because the physicians have the medical licenses.

That's not to say there isn't incredible pressure and expectations for employed physicians to refer patients to specific specialists and specific hospitals. Imagine that you are an employed family practice physician. You have an at-will employment contract that can be terminated at any time for no cause. In your employment contract is a standard noncompete clause, saying that you can't establish a competing practice or work for another group within a five-mile radius for two years after your employment is terminated. If you start referring patients to a competing imaging center or surgeons who don't practice at your employer's hospital, there is nothing to stop the hospital from terminating you. If you are terminated, you now have to find a job, or join another practice, that is located more than five miles away in every direction. For a family practice physician, five miles is another world. Five miles will mean the difference between 70% of your patients following you and 20% of your patients following you.

While employed physicians are still "technically" independent, there are very real, and very inconvenient, personal risks associated with biting the hand that feeds you. As a result, employed primary care physicians, and employed specialists, tend to behave very loyally to their employers.

Hospital administrators often refer to the challenge of trying to manage physicians as trying to "herd cats." How do you direct or control someone who doesn't work for you, and even if they do, they are legally licensed to make decisions you can't make? Physicians will often earn three to six times as much money as the middle managers and frontline managers who supervise the departments where they work. What's worse is that these managers are also dependent on these same physicians to refer and admit patients at their facility rather than other facilities.

The result is often policies and procedures that are very convenient for physicians but burdensome to hospital staff. A medical assistant for a hospital-affiliated cardiology group once told me that when the hospital started using electronic medical records, one of the cardiologists refused to stop using paper charts. He didn't want

---

to learn how to use the electronic medical record system. He was perfectly content with paper charts. He required all his support staff to continue filling out paper charts for his patients' visits *in addition to* charting patient visits electronically like the administration instructed them.

After the clinic's supervisor confronted the physician, she returned from the meeting, telling the staff to continue charting patient visits on both paper and the electronic system. The supervisor was in an impossible situation. She didn't have the training or the confidence to stand up for the staff, and this physician represented millions of dollars of hospital revenue. The independence of physicians and their ability to shift patient referrals to or away from any facility also makes hospital administrators very leery of investing in expensive equipment or facilities.

For example, as a hospital administrator, would you invest over $100,000 in a new set of surgical endoscopes for a single gastroenterologist who performs her procedures at three different hospitals in the area? She could stop treating patients at your hospital tomorrow and treat all of her patients at the other two facilities and there is nothing you could do about it. If she does shift referrals away from your facility, you will have a $100,000 piece of equipment that is practically worthless, because only gastroenterologists are medically licensed to use them.

Because physicians are independent, hospitals have to think long and hard about how they are going to mitigate the risk that their physicians could shift their patients to another facility. There are also stiff federal criminal laws against giving a physician any type of bribe to refer patients to you. The Anti-Kickback Statute has teeth, with criminal penalties of up to $25,000 per occurrence and five years in prison for the person giving the kickback.

So how do hospital administrators get comfortable making major purchases and investments if physicians can lackadaisically jump from hospital to hospital? I've observed three major mechanisms:

- **High quality service:** The most effective means of getting physicians to use your hospital and stay there, is also the most difficult to create. It takes years to put together a strong leadership team, middle-management staff, and workflow. There are thousands of operational metrics that have to be meticulously managed, including dropped-call ratios, medication error management, medical records, inventory, scheduling, surgical room turnaround times, infection control, labs, imaging, emergency department, intensive care, credentialing, and patient financial services.

- **Lease physician office space on campus:** Having a physician's office located on your campus creates a huge convenience factor for them to use your facility. Hospitals often offer physicians 10-to-15-year leases in medical office buildings connected to the hospital. However, this is difficult to do for several reasons. Physicians want affordable leases that are also attractive to patients and create a strong professional image. Affordable space and high-end building cosmetics are at opposite ends of the spectrum. Additionally, not only does it cost millions of dollars to build an office building, but practically all hospitals have them (with lots of empty, available space).

- **Doctor deals:** This is the quickest way to create a relationship with a physician. The hospital enters into a legal contract to have physicians perform professional services or become investment partners in some sort of business joint venture. The arrangements have to be genuine, legitimate business deals, not merely guises for giving physicians money.

Within the realm of commonly accepted legal arrangements, I have observed dozens of different types of doctor deals, business moves, if you will, that hospitals and health systems regularly use.

Physicians can always refer their patients to another facility, but these types of doctor deals are fairly effective in integrating and aligning the interests of physicians and hospitals.

VULNERABILITIES OF INDIVIDUAL PHYSICIANS AS SMALL BUSINESS OWNERS

Great chess players have devised specific strategies and tactics for the three phases of the game: the opening, the middle game, and the endgame.

The *opening* stage involves careful preparation, planning, and strategic positioning. Pieces positioned in the center of the board have more mobility and control, but they are also more exposed. Pieces positioned on the periphery and in corners are constrained and sometimes trapped.

The real action occurs in the *middle game*. The board opens up and so does the number of possible moves. As stated before, trying to plan your next four moves ahead could require you to consider 6.5 trillion possible variations. With such a broad array of moves, there is significant opportunity for creativity, strategy, and style. The board becomes a vast landscape—an ever-changing sea of possibilities.

In the *endgame*, when pieces have been taken, there is less material and resources to worry about. The creative aspects of the game melt away and raw logic takes over to govern the few pieces you have left. Garry Kasparov, the most enduring grandmaster of our time, calls the endgame "the treaty negotiation after the battle is over." When the general outcome is known, it is purely a mechanical exercise to work out the details, requiring little creativity.

These three phases are great analogies for the life cycles of hospitals, physician groups, and even the careers of individual physicians. Each begins with planning, careful preparation, and hard work. The *middle game* can vary significantly, depending on the strength of the *opening,* the ability to correctly predict the future, and the conviction to act on those beliefs. The *endgame* depends on the activities of the previous two stages.

An independent physician's opening stage is marked by diligent preparation and hard work. A physician spends seven years in medical school and residency.

Physicians may earn an MD or DO degree at one of 170 accredited medical schools in the United States. Of these accredited medical schools, MD degrees are issued by 141 of them and DO degrees are issued by 29 of them.

Of the 32 new medical schools accredited between 1912 and 2012, osteopathic (DO) schools accounted for 27 of them, while only five were allopathic (MD) schools. Between 15 and 20 new medical schools are projected to open between 2013 and 2015, with about half issuing MDs and half issuing DOs.

Medical schools in the United States and Canada only admit college graduates to a four-year didactic medical training program, while medical education in most other countries, including China and the United Kingdom, is offered as an undergraduate program. At the end of the four years of initial academic training, a medical degree is granted to the students.

Once the medical students graduate and get their degrees, they are well within their rights to "hang a shingle" and start practicing medicine without any additional training, though this has become something of a rarity. The majority of new doctors will enter medical residencies after graduation, marking the beginning of their specialization training.

Residencies vary based on the specialty, but there is a complicated matching system that takes place that calculates students' preferences and preceptors' assessments of students' aptitudes to match graduates to available residencies.

Internal medicine and family practice residencies are three years long, although residents may pursue further subspecialty training in such disciplines as cardiology, gastroenterology, geriatrics, pulmonology, and critical care medicine. Some residencies for other specialties, such as psychiatry, OBGYN, and orthopedics are three to five years long. Physicians in residencies are relatively capable but practice under the supervision of *attending physicians*, who basically double-check the residents' work and provide a safety net against errors.

Certain physicians, such as radiologists, may dedicate a full 10 to 12 years to completing their training, including four years of medical school, five years of residency, and one to three years of fellowship training.

Minimum Post-Graduate Residency / Fellowship Lengths

Hospital-Based Specialty	Years	Medical Specialty	Years	Surgical Specialty	Years
Anesth	4	Internal Med	3	Surgery	5
Emerg Med	3	Gastro	+3	Colorec	+1
Patho	3–4	Cardio	+3	Neuro	6–7
Radio	5	Intervent	+1	OBGYN	4
MSK	+1	Pulmon	+2	Ophth	3
ABD	+1	Crit Care	+2	Ortho	5
Nuc	+1	Family Med	3	Spine	+1
		Ped Intern	4	ENT	5
		Psychiatry	4	Plastic	3–6
				Urology	4–6

Source: Accreditation Council for Graduate Medical Education

Incidentally, radiologists are among the most highly compensated physicians, earning approximately $400,000 annually at the median and $600,000 at the 75ᵗʰ percentile.

Residencies are accredited by the Accreditation Council for Graduate Medical Education (ACGME). The ACGME has accredited residencies in 26 core areas with 96 subspecialties.

There are also 24 specialty board certification exams that physicians can take to affirm their specialty expertise after completing medical school, residencies, and fellowships. Specialized residency and fellowship training may be required to even sit for these exams, so not just any physician can sit for a board certification exam.

Each state also makes its own decisions regarding the recognition of training and credentials for foreign medical graduates who received their training in other countries.

A physician's *middle game*, like any professional career, is marked by a series of decisions about short-term and long-term issues. Included are thousands of day-to-day one-off decisions and major strategic decisions that will affect their practices for years into the future. Even when a decision is delayed or ignored, the indecisiveness in itself becomes a decision.

I have seen firsthand that a lack of foresight in planning for equipment replacements at physician-owned surgery and imaging centers often leads to more poor decision making in later years. Some hospital acquisitions of surgery centers and imaging centers are related, in part, to the previous owners' reluctance to fund or finance necessary replacement equipment when the existing equipment reached 10 to 12 years in age and needs to be replaced. I've worked on several transactions wherein the acquirers obtained MRIs, CT scanners, anesthesia machines, sterilizers, HVAC systems, endoscopy scopes, and surgical instrumentation that was well beyond their useful lives.

According to Dean Buonomano, author of *Brain Bugs*, the human brain is inherently not good at long-term planning. He calls this temporal myopia. People tend to choose to receive $100 today rather than $120 in thirty days, even though this equates to a 240% APR, far better than any return that could be made elsewhere. Humans are bad at judging how much time has elapsed, understanding risks, and calculating probabilities.

These shortcomings may have contributed in some respects to why hospital organizations now employ the vast majority of primary care physicians in the United States and an ever-growing proportion of physician specialists. By nature, physician practices tend to be fairly responsive to changes in their local markets, while hospital administrators tend to be somewhat captive to long-term plans. The effect is that physicians may have the nimbleness and speed to seize short-lived opportunities when they arise, but over the long run they also make mistakes, perhaps buying an office building that appears to be reasonably priced during a foreclosure sale, thinking that it is great deal, and assuming that they will grow into the space over time.

Hospitals tend to be more rigid. Big strategic decisions are made after many, many meetings, and they don't change easily. The rigidness and inability to respond quickly may mean that some opportunities are missed. However, if the big strategic decisions are good decisions, over the long run the hospital may be fine, even if it misses out here and there periodically.

This is a great analogy for professional gamblers and the casino. The casino dealers play blackjack with the rest of the players, but they are bound to play by the house's rules. The house may lose a hand here or there, but over the long haul, they always come out ahead. Casino managers don't sweat nervously every time some player goes on a hot streak. Over the long run, everything plays in the casino's favor. Organizations, as a group, seem to be better adapted to long-term planning, though they may be less responsive on a short-term basis.

For independent physician practices, there is a series of long-term strategic decisions each independent physician must make.

Office locations are a particularly important decision. Leases may be 10 years in length, thus making the consequences—good or bad—lasting. I have met many physicians who longed to move out of the cheap brick building where their current office is located into a shiny new medical office building with designer finishes, a luxurious common area with a water feature, and a view. They often told me that patients inherently perceive their service to be of a higher quality when the facility is of a higher quality.

On the opposite end of the real estate scale, I've met a number of physicians who invest heavily in real estate by buying the building where their office is located, buying a house and moving their office into it, or building a new building for themselves and sometimes other tenants.

This phenomenon was particularly evident with physicians in Florida. I went to the ocean side of Florida several times in 2009 to meet with surgeons to discuss a new surgery center and the opportunity for them to get block times there and even invest in the business. To my surprise, many surgeons were emphatic about the prospect of developing the surgery center in one or more medical office buildings they owned. I was in disbelief. Here I was, soft selling these surgeons on a medical facility, and the overwhelming response from many of them was that they could not afford to invest in it unless we located the business in one of their real estate facilities and signed a long-term lease. Who is selling whom?

Most of the surgeons I met with had lost money, serious money, on real estate and had no interest in jumping into another venture. In the classic story of the time, they had bought real estate with cash and debt, and they couldn't find tenants to rent the space out. No money was coming in, but they still had to service the debt they had borrowed to buy the buildings. They also couldn't sell the building because the real estate bubble burst and they were going to lose hundreds of thousands, or millions of dollars, on what they had paid for the properties.

Even those who just bought or developed space for their own practices, and not tenant space, often found that they had planned for growth that never materialized. I recently spoke with a physician who was selling his practice and becoming a hospital employee. I asked him why he wanted to sell, and part of his response was the fact that they had bought an office building that they were unable to rent or resell. "Do you need any office space?" he asked me.

Selecting office location and real estate is just one example of a decision that physicians must make. Other important ones are:

- Affiliations with hospitals, nursing homes, and other providers

- Call coverage services

- Medical director services

- Practice partner selection

- Compensation for physician employees and contractors

- Information systems and electronic medical records

- In-network and out-of-network contracting decisions

- Vendor relationships

- Subspecialty training to pursue

- Ancillary service equipment to acquire

- Staff management and development

- Employment of nurse practitioners and physician assistants

Each of these decisions has serious and important implications for an independent physician's professional practice.

Without question, the wealthiest physicians I have encountered made very predictable decisions with regard to the structure of their practice. For example:

- Their production levels were double the levels for their peers working at the 90th percentile.

- They relied heavily on nurse practitioners, physician assistants, and independent contractor physicians.

- They were extremely frugal with employed physician salaries—so much so that I often had to ask them how they convinced other physicians to work for so little.

- They owned multiple ancillary services and self-referred patients to them regularly, collecting hundreds of thousands of dollars per year through them. These services included businesses that provided DEXA scans, ultrasounds, EKGs, echocardiograms, vascular ultrasounds, MRIs, endoscopy centers, and retail orthotics.

- They hold multiple medical director positions at multiple facilities.

- They enter into extensive clinical management, coverage, and on-call agreements with hospitals.

The *endgame* for independent physicians may be characterized in several forms.

Some may see the endgame as retirement from private practice. The practice may continue to operate under the younger partners

---

who take over after their older partner retires. Or the retiring physician may sell the practice to another physician with whom he or she has not previously worked. This type of hand-off often involves the retiring physician staying on from six months to two years to assist with the transition of patients over to the new physician.

Another completely different type of *endgame* may occur when a group of physicians in the middle of their careers decides to sell its practice to a hospital or health system. These types of practice sales involve the selling physicians staying on as employed physicians and working for the health system, rather than being the owners of the practice. This type of practice sale is associated with stringent noncompete provisions, early termination provisions, and other legal mechanisms intended to keep the selling physicians from backing out of their sale and employment agreements.

The practice administrator of a large general surgery group once told me that the group's doctors had been offered a buyout by a major health system. They had discussed it at length and decided not to move forward with the sale. His advice to the group had been, "You can only kill the golden goose once." Many of the doctors were in their primes, with many more years of practice ahead of them. If they sold their practice, they would have no option but to be employees the rest of their careers in that community. The noncompete clauses would have forced them to relocate if they ever left the health system-owned practice.

My observation is that the sale of physician practices has become characterized by those who have no option but to sell and those who are nearing the latter half of their careers and are looking to cash in before retirement. Those with no other option are likely in financial distress related to one or more of the major decisions I mentioned earlier. Those looking to cash in before retirement plan to stay on just another five to 10 years while they transition the practice over to younger doctors who are earlier in their careers.

Chapter 2
Doctor Who?

OVERVIEW

This chapter discusses the following topics related to physicians in the United States:

- The Authoritative and Regulatory Organizations That Govern the Medical Profession

- The Distribution of Medical Specialties

- Hospitals and the Organizations that Regulate Them

- Example: A Start-Up Hospital's Reliance Upon Various Types of Physicians

- Surgeons

- A Few Words on Health Insurance

- The Value of Physician Consultations, Referrals, and Prescribed Orders

- Primary Care Physicians

- Physician Specialists

- Hospital Referrals and Consults

- Referral Web

THE AUTHORITATIVE AND REGULATORY ORGANIZATIONS THAT GOVERN THE MEDICAL PROFESSION

I've spent most of the last decade meeting and talking to physicians.

The medical profession in America, physicians, has a long history. If you want to read a very thorough, vivid history of the physician establishment, I recommend *The Social Transformation of American Medicine* by the Princeton sociologist Paul Starr. Since that book is over 500 pages, I will summarize the relevant points here in compact form.

In the 1800s, physician training was unregulated and un-accredited in the United States. Anyone could open a medical school and more or less sell medical degrees for money. As a result, there were a lot of quacks representing themselves as physicians. In the early 1900s the American Medical Association commissioned the Flexner Report, a study of the state of medical education in the United States. Eventually state medical boards stipulated that only graduates of accredited medical schools could identify themselves as physicians. It was also decided that the profession would be self-regulating. While the government set some high-level laws, physicians were responsible for training and policing each other's performance.

Physicians have always been a self-regulating profession. In the United States they regulate themselves at the state level with medical societies or state medical boards. The state-based boards, made up of physicians, issue medical licenses to graduates of accredited medical schools and take medical licenses away when deemed appropriate.

At the time of this book's publishing, there are 141 accredited medical schools in the United States and 17 in Canada accredited by the Liaison Committee on Medical Education (LCME) for MD degree programs, and 29 medical schools accredited by the American Osteopathic Association's Commission on Osteopathic College Accreditation (COCA) for DO degree programs. Most state boards of medical licensure require that U.S. medical schools be accredited by the LCME or the COCA, as a condition for licensure of their graduates. Eligibility of U.S. students to take the

United States Medical Licensing Examination (USMLE) requires accreditation of their school.[2]

While physicians may be sued in the courts for malpractice and other alleged medical errors, only the state medical boards can actually take away a physician's license to practice. Outside the courts, disciplinary action is imposed by fellow physicians because only other physicians are qualified to assess a physician's medical judgments.

The American Medical Association (AMA) is the national trade group for physicians in the United States. The AMA owns the patent on the current procedural terminology (CPT) medical coding system and also sets the weightings for the Relative Value Unit (RVU) scale every several years, on which most major physician reimbursement systems are based. RVUs measure and compare the relative amount of resources, including time, training, and office support, associated with all types of physician services.

The RVU system was invented in the mid-1980s by researchers at Harvard University. By the late 1980s the RVU system was included in the Omnibus Budget Reconciliation Act as the new basis for Medicare physician reimbursement. The Specialty Society Relative Value Scale Update Committee, also called the Relative Value Update Committee (RUC), is a committee of 25 physician specialists and six representatives from the AMA, the AOA, and several advisory organizations. The RUC was created by the AMA to periodically update the relative weights of the various physician services and procedures.

This independent committee of physicians establishes the comparative values for all physician services. The comparative values for the payment rates for all Medicare physician services, and subsequently most non-Medicare physician services, are based on this committee's decisions about the value associated with individual physician services.

When medical schools were first accredited, it was natural for them to associate themselves with hospitals. Hospitals in the United States in the 1800s were nothing like modern hospitals. In the 1700s and 1800s, physicians rode horseback and made house calls. Hospitals were typically more akin to "sick houses" maintained by nuns and religious institutions for the poor. Fast forward 150 years, and we see that many of the sick houses started by churches and religious orders still exist—but as modern hospitals.

Medical schools affiliated themselves with hospitals because they provided an ideal setting for studying and treating disease. There was no better place to find lots of sick people in one place. Over time, the evolution of medical specialists had major implications for the profession. Whereas physicians were originally generalists, the advent of hospital-based medical schools gave rise to physician specialists. While subspecialization was definitely an improvement for medicine, it resulted in divisive splits in the profession.

THE DISTRIBUTION OF MEDICAL SPECIALTIES

According to the Health Resources and Services Administration, an agency of the federal government's Department of Health and Human Services, the "physician supply will increase from current levels of approximately 817,000 active physicians under age 75 in 2005 to approximately 952,000 active physicians by 2020."[3]

According to the Association of American Medical Colleges' *2011 State Physician Workforce Data Book*, which was based on 2010 data, there were 799,509 active physicians in 2010.[4] The Association estimates that 92% to 93% of physicians have M.D. degrees and 7% to 8% have D.O. degrees.

According to my own personal analysis of the National Provider Identifier (NPI) database, I estimate there were approximately

842,000 physicians in the United States in 2012. Of this, I calculate that 47% of American physicians practice in one of three major specialty categories: internal medicine, family medicine, or pediatrics. It is worth mentioning, though, that internal medicine has nearly 19 subspecialties. For example, all cardiologists and gastroenterologists are internists with additional specialized training.

The NPI database indicates that about 31.5% of physicians in the United States are women and 68.5% are men.

While medical licensure (at the state level) sets the minimum standards for treating patients, board certification establishes specialty-specific training and competencies. There are 24 medical specialty boards that make up the American Board of Medical Specialties (ABMS). Most physicians who have completed specialized residency and fellowship training will seek board certification to establish their credentials in that specialty.

NPI Database Primary Medical Specialty Count

Primary Specialty	Count	Mix
Internal Medicine	206,370	25%
Family Medicine	110,659	13%
Pediatrics	74,859	9%
Psychiatry & Neurology	62,122	7%
Emergency Medicine	45,146	5%
Anesthesiology	44,886	5%
Obstetrics & Gynecology	41,876	5%
Radiology	40,342	5%
Surgery	35,482	4%
Orthopaedic Surgery	26,024	3%
Ophthalmology	18,853	2%
Podiatrist	17,074	2%
Pathology	16,775	2%
General Practice	12,658	2%
Dermatology	11,192	1%
Urology	10,306	1%
Otolaryngology	10,224	1%
Physical Medicine & Rehab	9,871	1%
Student-in-Training Program	6,055	1%
Neurological Surgery	5,703	1%
Hospitalist	5,028	1%

HOSPITALS AND THE ORGANIZATIONS THAT REGULATE THEM

Similarly, based on my personal inspection of the federal government's Medicare Cost Report database, I estimate that there are approximately 5,500 hospitals in the United States. Approximately 49% of these hospitals identify themselves as not-for-profit, while 28% identify themselves as proprietary, and 23% are government-owned. Additionally, 1,330 hospitals (24% of U.S. hospitals) are designated as rural, critical access hospitals with 25 beds or fewer. About half of U.S. hospitals have between 25 and 500 beds. Only about a dozen hospitals have more than 1,000 beds.

The American Hospital Association (AHA) states that there are approximately 5,724 hospitals, of which 4,973 are community hospitals. The rest are federal, psychiatric, and prison hospitals. The AHA indicates that 2,903 hospitals are not-for-profit, 1,025 are for-profit, and 1,045 are owned by local government.[5]

Hospitals, like all healthcare organizations, are regulated at the local, state, and federal levels. At the local city or county level, they must comply with life and safety building regulations established by the county engineers and the fire marshal. Hospitals are licensed at the state level by the state department of health. At the federal level, if a hospital wants to accept Medicare patients (nearly all do) it will probably seek accreditation via The Joint Commission (TJC), formerly known as the Joint Commission on Accreditation of Healthcare Organizations. Medicare "deems" that accredited healthcare facilities have satisfied the health and safety standards component of Medicare certification. In other words, if your facility obtains accreditation through TJC, then Medicare will automatically grant your facility Medicare certification without needing to have Medicare's own surveyors come to your facility.

Under the federal Emergency Medical Treatment and Active Labor Act (EMTALA), hospitals participating in the Medicare program are required to operate an emergency department and to provide diagnostic and medical stabilization services to patients requiring medically emergent services regardless of patients' ability to pay. They are not legally required to provide medical care to non-emergent patients.

At a minimum, a hospital usually has an emergency room, an inpatient floor with beds, and operating rooms.

Not-for-profit hospitals are tax-exempt, meaning that they do not have to pay state or federal income taxes, although they may still have to pay property taxes or other specific taxes depending on their state. Not-for-profit hospitals generally operate as tax-exempt organizations under one of the eligible tax-exempt purposes identified by the IRS.

The most common exempt purposes used are "health promotion" and "educational institutions." Health promotion is a broad term that may be justified by the hospital's provision of uncompensated charity care, free clinic services, free prevention screening services, free health education services, or other similar social services that might otherwise have to be provided by the government. The educational tax-exempt purpose may apply to hospitals affiliated with university medical centers where medical schools are operated and medical students are being trained.

Hospital Administration

The hospital CEO job is highly political by nature. It is a high-profile position partly because it is so well compensated. The average salary is about $400,000 a year at a medium-size hospital and $600,000 for a large hospital or small health system. The salary is high, of course, because so few people can do the job very well for any length of time. Accordingly, the turnover for the top position is also very high. The average tenure for a hospital CEO is about 3.5 years.

As with any leadership position, the candidate becomes the target of a lot of judgment and criticism for everyday decisions. If there are three possible choices for a problem, Option A, Option B, and doing nothing, each possible decision will have proponents and critics. Option A may be supported by 80% of the staff. Meanwhile, 10% of the staff are indifferent, and 10% of the staff are opposed to Option A. Simultaneously, 75% of the staff may be indifferent to Option B, while 20% are supportive, and only 5% are opposed.

No matter what choice leadership makes, someone is going to be unhappy. Often there are supercritics who will disapprove no matter what the leadership says or does. Of course, there is nothing anyone can do to appease these types of critics.

What makes the job difficult is that big decisions have to be made every day and often. The important decisions, of which there are many, work their way upstream because no one wants to make difficult decisions downstream.

The consequences of all these decisions are also highly political because important physicians in many health systems are still independent. If they are unhappy with the way their hospital is being operated, they can start treating all their patients at the next closest hospital. This physician independence is good from the perspective that physicians aren't locked in to treating patients in an environment that would be unsafe for them. But it is extremely frustrating for a hospital administrator who is constantly being threatened financially by his or her main referral sources disagreeing with how the organization is being operated.

Academic Medicine, Teaching Hospitals, Faculty, and Residents

Perhaps the most complicated subsector of healthcare is the one that includes academic medical centers. They combine two of the most political and complex organizations—universities and hospitals—into large, unwieldy conglomerations.

Academic medical centers often have sophisticated employment arrangements with faculty physicians who may be employed by the university, the hospital, a joint venture, or a combination thereof, with or without some elements of independent practice. Unlike the independent physician in practice, the academic physician may have teaching responsibilities, research responsibilities, and publication responsibilities, and may serve in one or more administrative directorship roles for various departments at both the university and the hospital. It is fairly common for several departments of the hospital organization to each reimburse the university or a joint venture for specific components of a faculty physician's salary.

For example, a faculty physician employed by the university may be subsidized by the hospital for the two directorships she fulfills as well as on-call coverage she takes about two days per month. Two to three different hospital departments may pay back the university for 30% to 50% of the faculty physician's salary.

Teaching Hospitals

A hospital can still be a teaching hospital without being an academic medical center. A teaching hospital is a facility that hosts medical residencies for training physicians. According to the Association for American Medical Colleges (AAMC), there are nearly 400 teaching hospitals hosting residencies for graduates of medical colleges in the United States and Canada.[6]

Teaching hospitals that are not academic medical centers have missions to primarily provide health services to the communities they serve. Teaching and training residents is a secondary priority to their community service mission.

In contrast, some would say that academic medical centers' primary mission is research and resident training, with community service being a secondary priority. This interpretation is not meant to be disparaging to academic medical centers. They certainly provide a disproportionate share of medical services to uninsured and indigent care populations.

Teaching hospitals, where resident training is a secondary priority, still maintain resident programs to supplement emergency department on-call coverage, unassigned inpatient management, and as a device for physician recruitment.

My experience with on-call coverage arrangements is that the residents are always supervised by attending physicians, so their work is being double-checked for accuracy.

Residents

Medical residents in the United States are an interesting topic of debate. While residents are licensed physicians with medical degrees, many believe they are overworked during the critical residency phase of their training. In the United States, the ACGME prohibits a residency program from utilizing a medical resident over 88 hours per week. This is a significantly longer work week than that of European medical residents, who are limited to a 48-hour work week.

A 2005 study by researchers at Brown Medical School (now The Warren Alpert Medical School of Brown University) published in the *Journal of the American Medical Association* compared pediatric medical residents who had just performed a heavy call coverage rotation (80 to 90 hours per week) to being intoxicated with a blood alcohol level of 0.04 to 0.05 g% (per 100 mL of blood).[7] The study compared the driving abilities of the 34 test subjects using a simulator. The researchers concluded that residents on heavy call rotations exhibited similar performance to the intoxicated group. What is perhaps just as concerning is that both groups were found to have limited abilities to even recognize their own performance issues.

So not only are sleep-deprived residents just as incapable as drunk residents, they are just as unlikely to recognize how poorly they are performing while they are sleep-deprived. Some commentators dispute the study by pointing out that the sleep-deprived residents were prohibited from taking caffeine stimulants during the study, as many residents do.

Residency sites and hospitals contend that not only are the hour requirements intended to teach residents how to think when they are tired, but that residents are inherently very inefficient, taking much longer to perform basic medical tasks than normal physicians.

EXAMPLE: A START-UP HOSPITAL'S RELIANCE UPON VARIOUS TYPES OF PHYSICIANS

The *doctor deal* decisions that have to be made when starting a new hospital are consistent with our metaphor of critical opening plays in chess. These decisions can have lasting consequences.

If you were going to start a new hospital, there are a few physician coverage arrangements you need: You must be TJC-accredited, state-licensed, and Medicare-certified. This applies to even the smallest 25-bed hospital.

At a minimum, you will probably need:

1. 24/7 emergency medicine physician coverage for the emergency department.

2-8. 24/7 on-call ED coverage for OBGYN, pediatrics, general surgery, orthopedic surgery, cardiology, and neurology. There are other specialties too, but these are the key basic ones.

9. Radiologist interpretation coverage for all imaging studies. This may be provided through a combination of local radiologist coverage during the day and remote night time coverage ("Nighthawk").

10.   Anesthesiologist coverage for all surgery and deliveries, whether elective or emergent.

11.   Pathologist coverage for all lab tests.

That's eleven physician coverage agreements you need just to open the door to your tiny 25-bed hospital. As your start-up hospital becomes more successful and adds more beds and more services, even more coverage arrangements will be necessary. First you might add:

12.   An additional 75 inpatient medical/surgical beds. Now you need to secure more internal medicine and family physicians to round on unassigned inpatients. Patients admitted through the emergency department may not have a physician to oversee their care. Your hospital will have to assign "hospitalists" to consult with specialists and oversee those patients' care.

13.   A 10-bed pediatric inpatient unit. Specialty pediatric care requires you to engage pediatricians to constantly round on all unassigned pediatric inpatients.

14.   A cardiac catheterization laboratory. Interventional cardiologists have to be on call 24/7 who are able and willing to show up within 30 minutes of being called for heart attack patients.

15.   A 15-bed intensive care unit. A continuous coverage contract has to be established with a critical care physician group.

After several years of providing these second tier services, everything has been working out pretty well, and you're ready to add some pretty sophisticated service lines, including:

16.   Another 100 inpatient beds. You're now ready to contract with dedicated, full-time physician hospitalists to provide

on-site medical coverage to your inpatients.

17. A stroke program. Now you need interventional neurologists who can show up within 30 minutes anytime of the day.

18. A hospice and palliative care program. Now you need palliative care physicians to consult on inpatient and home health patients.

19. A world-class open-heart surgery program. Now you need cardiac surgeons to help you buy all the equipment, develop protocols, and develop the surgical nursing staff to do coronary artery bypass grafts, Da Vinci robotic surgery, and heart transplants.

20. A neonatal intensive care unit (NICU) for newborns. Now you need to engage a neonatology physician group to provide 24/7 coverage, buy all your equipment, and direct the neonatal nurse practitioners you're going to hire.

21. A pediatric intensive care unit (PICU) with pediatric critical care physicians providing 24/7 coverage.

At this point you have 21 agreements with various physician groups just to ensure physicians will show up to treat patients who present in emergency situations. You should also have a medical director for each service area, so at least another 20 or so physician contracts will be executed to formalize medical directors to set policies and standards for care provided in each service line.

SURGEONS

Lest we not forget all the local surgeons who have to decide where they will perform surgery. Aside from outpatient surgery joint ventures, which we will discuss later, you have to compete with other local hospitals and surgery centers as the destination of choice for surgery.

Let us assume that your hospital has six operating rooms and four delivery rooms. There are about 80 surgeons in the community who have been credentialed and granted privileges to use your facility for surgery. About 60 of the 80 surgeons would prefer to perform surgery at 7:00 a.m. in the morning on weekdays. That way they can get three to five surgeries done by lunch.

However, because you only have six operating rooms, and no one does elective surgery on the weekends, you only have 30 7:00 a.m. start times during the week. Most of the surgeons want to schedule their surgeries in three to five patient "blocks" once or twice per week. So right off the bat, 30 of the 60 surgeons wanting 7:00 a.m. start times are going to be disappointed. How do you choose which surgeons will get the 7:00 a.m. start times?

Would you perhaps give the 7:00 a.m. start times to the busiest surgeons who are in a position to bring the most business to your hospital? There would certainly be benefits to getting friendly with the power surgeons in the community. A productive orthopedic surgeon could potentially perform 200 to 300 surgeries or more over a year. At $10,000 to $30,000 a pop, one *busy* surgeon could easily generate revenues between $2,000,000 and $10,000,000 a year for a hospital.

However, giving priority scheduling to physicians, or any form of consideration, based on the volume or value of patient referrals, could be construed as a violation of the Anti-Kickback Statute. While your hospital is not giving the surgeon cash, you are giving the surgeon something of value with the specific intent to induce that surgeon to admit more patients to your hospital and not the other hospital in town.

Also, many of the surgeons want to book two operating rooms

---

at a time so they can "bounce" back and forth between the two rooms. They want two rooms because they could have to wait 30 minutes while each operating room "turned-over" and re-sterilized. They would much prefer to have their next patient ready in the operating room next door so they can re-sterilize and promptly proceed into the next surgery.

This may be the best use of the surgeon's time, but it is horrible for your hospital from an operational and financial perspective. When you give a surgeon two rooms, you have empty operating rooms sitting while they are using the other one. This is a waste of valuable schedule time. Operating rooms are tremendously expensive to develop. The building costs can frequently exceed $300 a square foot for all the special electricity, lighting, gas piping, flooring, and environmental systems associated with operating room requirements. From a purely business perspective, it is not sound to have such expensive assets sitting unused. In this respect, your hospital's need to keep operating rooms continuously scheduled during weekdays is counter to individual surgeons' needs to have two operating rooms available to them on their surgery day.

A FEW WORDS ON HEALTH INSURANCE

The focus of this book is not health insurance, nor does the reader necessarily have to be familiar with insurance to understand the concepts in this book. However, because it is an important part of the American healthcare system, some fundamental health insurance topics are discussed here.

Health insurance is a type of risk-pooling through which a large number of people share the risk that a few of them may get sick by pooling some of their money (premiums) and setting it aside to pay for medical costs when someone does incur medical costs.

Medical insurance works because the incidence of disease, or the number of people who will get sick, is fairly predictable within large populations. For example, we may be able to estimate with reasonable accuracy that of 100,000 randomly selected people, 7% of the them will get the flu within a one-year period, 20% of them will use prescription medication, 1.5% of them will break a bone, 5% of them will give birth, 1% of them will contract cancer, and 0.5% of them will die.

While we can't necessarily guess who exactly will get sick, this predictability of disease makes it fairly easy to estimate the costs of the medical care needed for that group of people over one year, and subsequently we can predict how much each person should have to pay in premiums to cover all the medical costs that will be incurred over the next year.

In the United States, most health insurance has been provided to employed working people as an employer-sponsored benefit, whereby employers pay 70% to 90% of health insurance premiums for their employees. The federal government has sponsored Medicare health insurance for persons over 65 years of age, while states and the federal government have sponsored Medicaid health insurance for uninsured persons living near the federal poverty level. Medicaid primarily benefits children in poor families and elderly people in nursing homes.

There has been a long-standing debate in the United States about whether providers should be compensated using a fee-for-service model or a capitated, population-based model. The fee-for-service model pays medical providers for each individual service rendered. Therefore, the more services providers render, the more they get paid. The capitated, population-based model might pay a physician a fixed monthly rate, for example, $60 per member per month to manage the health of thousands of patients. If the physician can provide all the care needed for less than the fees paid to him or her, then the physician can keep the balance of the fees paid. If the physicians incur more costs providing care than what is paid, the physician will lose money. The capitated model inherently encourages physicians to ration services because it puts physicians at risk for the cost of care, while the fee-for-service model does not put physicians at risk.

THE VALUE OF PHYSICIAN CONSULTATIONS, REFERRALS, AND PRESCRIBED ORDERS

A *consultation (or a consult)* is defined as one physician specialist providing his or her professional advice to another physician regarding a patient of the latter physician. The consulting physician provides his or her professional opinion, while the patient's primary physician is responsible for the patient's care.

A *referral* is defined as the transfer of a patient's care from one provider to another. A physician can refer a patient to another physician or to a hospital or medical facility.

A *physician order* is required to access prescription medication and many types of ancillary services. The physician order signifies that a treatment is medically necessary, which is a core requirement for insurance coverage and payment. So while I could probably pay cash and get an MRI for no reason, for my insurance to pay for the MRI, a physician must order it based on some sort of medical need for an MRI.

Referrals and physician orders are worth quite a bit of money to the recipients. Medical facilities, ancillary providers, drug companies, pharmacies, therapy practices, nursing homes, and device companies are all competing for patient referrals and physician orders.

PRIMARY CARE PHYSICIANS

Just three major physician specialties (excluding subspecialties) make up 47% of all physicians. This includes family practice physicians, internal medicine physicians, and pediatricians. These specialties represent the base of the medical referral pyramid. Whereas specialists may only see a particular patient a few times, primary care sees large volumes of patients repeatedly over many years. Primary care physicians exert considerable influence as a group. On an annual basis American primary care physicians:

1. Refer millions of patients to hospital emergency departments and inpatient units;

2. Order millions of drug prescriptions for their patients;

3. Order millions of laboratory and imaging tests; and

4. Refer millions of patients to physician specialists.

Additionally, primary care physicians, as a whole, are closely tied to hospitals on a large scale by:

1. Rounding on millions of patients in hospital settings.

2. Providing millions of hours of on-call emergency department coverage.

3. Providing millions of hours of medical director services.

These activities are shown in the following illustration.

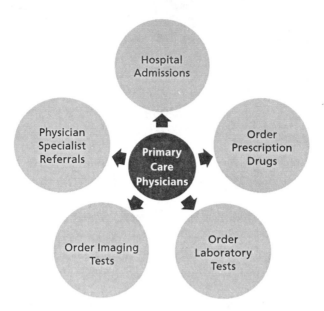

What is notable about primary care physicians is that they are not reliant on other providers or physicians for receiving patient referrals. Primary care physicians refer patients to a wide array of other physicians, facilities, and services, but no one refers patients to primary care physicians. Primary care is the base of the referral pyramid. Many other healthcare providers are reliant on primary care for patient referrals, but primary care only relies on their existing patients for referring new patients to them.

Despite wielding so much power from a referral standpoint, in most markets there are few large independent primary care physician groups. Rather than consolidate the many small primary care practices into larger professional organizations, the trend has been for primary care physicians to seek employment at hospital-affiliated groups, which are not owned by physicians.

Large primary care physician groups are at the core of many successful health systems and HMOs.

PHYSICIAN SPECIALISTS

Physician specialists, depending on the specialty, exercise different types of referral influence than primary care, while some specialists, such as anesthesiologists, pathologists, and radiologists, have minimal patient referral power. That is not to say that limited ability to refer patients makes such physicians any less important or less valued. Later I will discuss how I believe anesthesiologists are perhaps the most influential physicians in hospitals.

The next illustration shows the patient referral power that an orthopedic surgeon exercises. While orthopedic surgeons and primary care physicians both have the ability to order prescription drugs, to order imaging tests, and to admit patients to hospitals, orthopedic surgeons can also refer patients to outpatient surgery centers, pain management physicians, and physiatrists, as well as physical therapists.

Orthopedic surgeons are also in a position to select the implantable screws, plates, and artificial knees and hips used in their surgeries. Orthopedic surgeons do not purchase the implantable devices used in their surgeries, however. The hospital or surgery center has to buy them from the manufacturer. Orthopedic surgeons may also send patients home with crutches, slings, casts, or other types of durable medical equipment that is reimbursed by insurance.

The patient's insurance company has to compensate the hospital or surgery center for these devices. The patient's employer and the patient are ultimately paying these costs through health insurance premiums, deductibles, and coinsurances.

For this reason, drug manufacturers, imaging centers, hospitals, surgery centers, pain management physicians, physical therapists, physiatrists, post-acute home health and skilled nursing facilities, and medical device manufacturers are all reliant on orthopedic surgeons for patient referrals. It does not take much imagination to realize the serious implications that the Stark self-referral law and Anti-Kickback Statute have in the U.S. healthcare system. While the Anti-Kickback Statute prohibits paying or receiving anything to induce referrals or generate federal health care program business, the Stark Law (42 U.S.C. §1395nn) broadly prohibits physicians from making referrals to an entity for the furnishing of designated health services (DHS) payable by Medicare, if the physician or an immediate family member of the physician has a financial relationship with the entity.[8] The Stark Law is discussed further in the next chapter.

This same pattern of patient referrals holds true for most medical and surgical physician specialists, though it applies in different ways.

For example, an imaging center with an MRI is going to be very reliant on orthopedic surgeons, an imaging center with ultrasound is going to very reliant on OBGYNs, and an imaging center with a CT scanner is going to be very reliant on internal medicine physicians. Similarly, physical therapists rely on orthopedic surgeons, speech therapists rely on neurologists and pediatricians, and audiologists rely on otolaryngologists.

HOSPITAL REFERRALS AND CONSULTS

Hospital services have to be ordered by physicians. It is odd to believe that million dollar and billion dollar organizations frequently rely on independent third-parties to tell them what services they can or can't provide to their customers. Can you imagine if independent consultants decided what you needed when you went to the grocery store? How frustrating would it be for Wal-Mart to know that an independent consultant would dictate what services and products they were allowed to sell to each of their customers?

A hospital *admission* is really just a physician deeming it is necessary for a patient to receive treatment at a hospital and spending the night. An overnight stay characterizes the treatment as an inpatient stay. If the patient needs hospital treatment, but does not need to stay overnight, his or her treatment is considered to be an outpatient treatment.

Hospitals, while traditionally on the receiving end of physician referrals, also refer patients out as well. Hospital discharge planners may help select post-acute healthcare providers like home health agencies, skilled nursing facilities, inpatient rehabilitation facilities, long-term care hospitals, and long-term care nursing homes. Hospitals may also facilitate patient referrals to physicians through on-call arrangements and consults.

If a patient presents in the emergency room and a physician specialist is consulted via phone or in person, there is a chance the patient may become the specialist physician's patient. The ideal on-call event is a five-minute telephone call during which the emergency medicine physician describes the patient's symptoms to the specialist. The specialist determines he or she does not need to see the patient immediately and instructs the patient to schedule an appointment with their office during normal hours.

An inpatient consult, which also may be via phone or in person, may involve the hospitalist requesting input from a physician specialist without necessarily transferring the patient's care to the specialist. An example would be a hospitalist consulting a pain management physician or infectious disease physician. Inpatient consults are billable events. The consulting physician can bill the patient's insurance for his or her time and input.

REFERRAL WEB

Imagine the complicated web of referrals among healthcare providers. Patients are constantly being referred from their primary care physicians to specialists. All physicians are constantly ordering lab tests, imaging scans, and prescription drugs. From the following chart it is no wonder that Health Maintenance Organizations (HMOs) put primary care physicians in charge of all patient referrals. The primary care physician refers patients to everyone, but no one refers patients to primary care physicians.

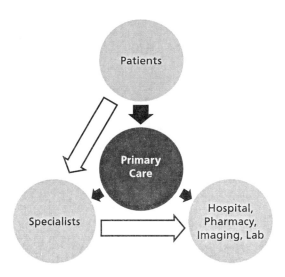

What is more interesting is the evolution of patient self-referral to specialists. Much information is available via the Internet, and health insurance company websites in particular, about medical conditions and diseases. Millions of patients are diagnosing their own diseases, just as a primary care physician would, and then self-referring themselves to orthopedists, podiatrists, dermatologists, allergists, physiatrists, and other specialists. This self-referral tendency is permissible in Preferred Provider Organization (PPO) health plans, which do not require a primary care referral to see a specialist.

Chapter 3:
Joint-Venture Deals

OVERVIEW

This chapter discusses the following topics related to business joint ventures with physicians:

- Examples: Common Types of Physician–Hospital Joint Ventures

- The Rise and Fall of HealthSouth

- The Stark Laws, Designated Health Services, and the Exceptions

- The Anti-Kickback Statute and the Safe Harbors

- Joint Venture Governance and Operating Agreement Terms

- Joint-Venture Life Cycle

- Surgery Centers and Endoscopy Centers

- Imaging Centers

- Specialty/Surgical Hospitals

- Dialysis/Vascular Access Centers

- Management and Co-Management with Physicians

- Cardiac Catheterization Labs

- Radiation Therapy Centers

EXAMPLES: COMMON TYPES OF PHYSICIAN–HOSPITAL JOINT VENTURES

Joint ventures are one of the most effective devices for aligning hospitals and physicians. In the typical joint venture, the hospital and a group of physicians invest in a business together. The joint venture may be either a newly formed business, a business that was previously owned by the physicians, or a business that was previously owned by the hospital. I spent the first four-and-a-half years of my career exclusively working on physician–hospital joint ventures.

Experience has taught me that joint ventures rarely involve the partners sitting around a campfire singing "Kumbaya." In many cases, one of the parties was more or less *blackmailed* into entering in the joint venture as a defensive move. Dozens of times I've heard, "It is better to own 50% of something than 100% of nothing."

Here are several illustrations of joint ventures:

- St. Mary's Hospital and Advanced Radiology Associates develop a new diagnostic imaging center. The radiologists do not have enough capital to develop the imaging center entirely by themselves, and the hospital has a master land lease on the medical office building. The imaging center signs a 15-year lease in a medical office building. The hospital owns 60% of the new imaging center, and the radiologists own 40%. The owners split the profits 60–40, according to the ownership split.

- General Hospital buys a 60% interest in a business called Advanced Surgical Center (ASC). Prior to the hospital's investment, ASC was owned entirely by a group of 17 surgeons. The business was overbuilt. The owners believe hospital affiliation will improve primary care referrals from hospital-employed physicians and that hospital-affiliated surgeons will be more likely to perform surgeries at the facility. The hospital realigns itself with several physicians who shifted their surgical cases away from the hospital operating rooms to this surgery center.

- Good Samaritan Hospital builds a new medical office building connected to its new hospital facility. The hospital invites physicians who will rent office space there to invest in the medical office building. The physicians' effective office space lease rate is lower, because they are paying *themselves* to some extent. Over the 10-year lease term, the physicians save considerably on their office leases by being owners in the building.

- Methodist Hospital has a freestanding, outpatient surgical center near its campus. The surgical center was purchased from several physicians many years ago, and it is now operated under the hospital's tax identification number as a department of the hospital. Mostly eye surgeries are performed there. Several orthopedic surgeons on the hospital's staff want to turn the facility back into an ambulatory surgery center and operate it as a joint venture with the hospital. The hospital has a Fair Market Value appraisal opinion performed for the business. The hospital contributes the old facility and cash to the joint venture and the physicians contribute cash. The ownership split is based on the relative value of each investor's overall financial contribution.

THE RISE AND FALL OF HEALTHSOUTH

HealthSouth Corporation was the unofficial pioneer of physician joint-ventured outpatient surgery and imaging centers. At its height in 2000, HealthSouth operated more ambulatory surgery centers (ASCs) and imaging centers collectively than any single healthcare organization has before or since. As of December 31, 2000, HealthSouth operated 222 ASCs and 136 imaging centers, not to mention a number of inpatient rehabilitation hospitals and therapy businesses

By comparison, 14 years later, the largest ASC operators— Amsurg, USPI, and SCA—each operate 242, 214, and 171 ASCs, respectively, but no imaging centers. In imaging, Radnet, Inc. and Alliance Healthcare Services, Inc. are now the only major operators left, with 250 and 125 imaging centers, respectively, but no surgery centers.[9,10] None of the for-profit or not-for-profit hospital systems are even close to the ambulatory market share that HealthSouth had. HCA[11] is the largest hospital operator of ASCs, with 115 in 2014.

HealthSouth's joint ventures with physicians were effectively disruptive to hospitals and health systems. HealthSouth created free-standing medical facilities in partnership with physicians that subsequently provided low-risk, low-cost surgery and imaging services to patients, insurance, and employers. Their physician surgeon partners admitted surgery patients to their ASCs rather than the hospitals where they formerly performed surgery, while radiologists were equally amenable to receiving an interpretation fee for reading at an outpatient imaging center or a hospital.

An equal or greater number of joint ventures between hospital and physicians was likely created as defensive responses to HealthSouth's success. Virtually all of the surgeries and imaging scans performed at the 5,300 ASCs and 6,800[12] imaging centers in the United States used to be performed in hospital settings.

If HealthSouth's founder and CEO Richard Scrushy had not been repeatedly indicted by federal prosecutors for fraud, racketeering, money laundering, bribery, and various other crimes by the FBI and SEC,[13,14] HealthSouth could have established itself as the dominant healthcare system for decades.

HealthSouth's original CFO, Aaron Beam recounted the story of the company in the book *HealthSouth: The Wagon to Disaster.* Beam met Scrushy in 1980 when they both worked at the hospital management company Lifemark. When American Medical International (AMI) bought Lifemark in 1983, Scrushy procured $1 million from Citicorp venture capitalists to start a chain of outpatient therapy centers.

His business plan was to provide outpatient services to patients at lower costs than what was provided in hospital settings through more convenient outpatient settings. The icing on the cake was their idea of letting physicians invest in the centers. This was key to the business model because it was the physicians who ordered the services. HealthSouth retained at least 51% of each of their centers so they could consolidate all their financial statements.

Outpatient healthcare services were cutting edge in the early 1980s. Medicare just started making payments to ASCs and Comprehensive Outpatient Rehabilitation Facilities (CORFs) in the early 1980s.

The new company was founded in 1984. Scrushy corralled a number of physicians in Little Rock, Arkansas, to start the company's first center.

A short time later Citicorp was joined by First Century Partners, Smith Barney, William Blair Venture Partners, and Allstate Insurance in a second fundraising round of $6 million. Scrushy and Beam were invited to speak at investment banking conferences on healthcare, where they received exposure to mutual funds, banks, pension funds, and other investors.

Scrushy realized that the services provided by rehabilitation hospitals and skilled nursing facilities (SNFs) were very similar. The company opened its first inpatient rehabilitation hospital in Florence, South Carolina, by acquiring a newly constructed

88-bed SNF and re-licensing it as an inpatient facility. At the time, in 1984, there were only 55 rehabilitation hospitals in the United States, but similar to the modern payment mechanisms, the inpatient rehabilitation hospitals received five times as much revenue as outpatient rehabilitation facilities because of the higher level of service they provided.

In 1985 the original name of the company, Amcare, was changed to HealthSouth to differentiate it from its competitors.

The company planned to hold a public offering in 1986 when it was first projected to become profitable. In the summer of 1986, it engaged Robertson Colman & Stephens, Drexel Burnham Lambert, and Alex Brown & Sons as their investment bankers and filed their S-1 with the Securities and Exchange Commission (SEC) in September of 1986. On September 24, 1986, the stock began trading on the NASDAQ. Two million shares were issued at approximately $6.50 per share, and the market price rose to $10 per share within a few days. By October of 1987, the stock had risen to $16 per share. Beam estimates that Scrushy's net worth rose to over $100 million by the early 1990s.

By the end of 1995, HealthSouth had $1.6 billion in annual revenues and 26,000 employees. It also had the highest price-to-earnings ratio of any company in its sector.

Despite all its growth, Beam claimed that Scrushy refused to report the bad numbers when HealthSouth was not going to meet Wall Street expectations in the second quarter of 1996. Bill Owens, the HealthSouth controller, made numerous journal entries, each less than $5,000, to improve the appearance of HealthSouth's performance during that quarter. He did this again when performance did not improve during the third quarter of 1996 and subsequently in 1997. Aaron Beam left HealthSouth voluntarily in mid-1997, announcing that he would retire at age 54.

By 2002, the fraudulent bookkeeping had snowballed. The reality of HealthSouth's financial performance diverged further and further from the picture reported by the company as growth expectations continued to rise on top of more and more doctored financials. Approximately 120,000 falsified journal entries per quarter were required to maintain the deceit. HealthSouth reported to have $320 million in cash at one time while it actually only had $10 million.

Despite this, HealthSouth maintained a fleet of 10 corporate aircraft that the company staff nicknamed "Air Birmingham."

Scrushy personally had six homes in his name, 37 cars, jets, a seaplane, a helicopter, a yacht, and numerous boats. In 2001, Scrushy purchased an 11,000-sq.-ft. home in Palm Beach, Florida, valued at $11 million. He also owned a 14,000-sq.-ft., $5 million Lake Martin home, and a 16,000-sq.-ft. Vestavia Hills home valued at $2.2 million. The most flamboyant of his cars included a $250,000 Lamborghini and a $135,000 bullet-proof BMW.

In July of 2002, Congress passed Sarbanes-Oxley into law. This law required the CEO and CFO to personally certify financial statements. The then-current HealthSouth CFO, Weston Smith, who was well aware of the ongoing fraud, was very reluctant to personally certify the financial statements. The new regulations carried penalties of up to 20 years in prison. Weston was also getting married that month.

Ten days before the certification statement was due in August of 2002, Weston Smith physically left the HealthSouth building and notified its officers that he was not coming back.

Scrushy convinced Weston Smith to return and sign the certifications under the agreement that they would spin off the surgery center company, which was not wrought with fraud, and Weston and Scrushy would become CFO and CEO of that company. The failing financial performance of HealthSouth proper would then be attributed to concurrent Medicare reimbursement cuts affecting the entire therapy industry. Their plan was to take advantage of the depressed HealthSouth stock price by privatizing it in a leveraged buyout. Weston was convinced that the shareholders would benefit from the sale of the surgery center business.

The fall of the company was ultimately triggered by the fact that Scrushy cashed in $100 million in stock options just prior to the announcement of the company changes. This timing was questioned by many shareholders who were in disbelief that this was a coincidence.

Weston Smith subsequently began working with the FBI, the U.S. Attorney's office, the SEC, and the IRS to help them build a case for prosecuting the various forms of fraud that had been committed.

On March 18, 2003, the FBI raided HealthSouth's corporate offices. The next day, Weston Smith entered into a plea arrangement. The subsequent CFO, Bill Owens, also pleaded guilty to fraud and CEO Richard Scrushy was dismissed by HealthSouth's Board of Directors.

In November of 2003, Scrushy was indicted on 85 counts of fraud, including wire fraud, money laundering, conspiracy, and making false statements. Scrushy was the first CEO charged under the Sarbanes-Oxley Act. The federal government seized Scrushy's assets and his bail was set at $10 million.

While Scrushy was initially acquitted on all 36 of the accounting fraud counts against him, the company had to engage the restructuring firm Alvarez & Marsal and appointed Bryan Marsal as Chief Restructuring Officer. By the end of 2003, the company had most of its finances reorganized and was able to avoid Chapter 11 bankruptcy.

The board of directors of HealthSouth sold all but a few of the company's 11 corporate jets.

On March 26, 2007, HealthSouth announced it would sell its surgery center division to TPG Capital for $920 million in cash and a $25 to $30 million dollars equity interest in the newly formed company that the surgery division would become. The surgery center division comprised 139 outpatient surgery centers and three surgical hospitals. The transaction was completed on June 30, 2007. The new surgery center business was named Surgical Care Affiliates.

On April 29, 2007, HealthSouth announced an agreement to sell its diagnostic division to the Gores Group for $47.5 million dollars. The transaction was completed on July 31, 2007. The diagnostic company was named Diagnostic Health Corporation.

What happened at HealthSouth was a true tragedy. HealthSouth had a major head start on what has become a huge subsector of the healthcare industry. It practically invented the physician joint venture business model. If the company had been more frugal with its discretionary expenses and not engaged in years of accounting fraud, there is no telling how successful it could have been.

THE STARK LAWS, DESIGNATED HEALTH SERVICES, AND THE EXCEPTIONS

There are many restrictions imposed on physicians regarding the types of businesses in which they are allowed to invest. These federal Stark Law investment restrictions are intended to prevent physicians from making medical decisions based on their own personal financial gain. For example, physicians cannot invest in the following businesses if they refer patients to them:

- Clinical laboratory services

- Physical therapy, occupational therapy, and speech language pathology services

- Radiology and certain other imaging services

- Radiation therapy services and supplies

- Durable medical equipment and supplies

- Parenteral and enteral nutrients, equipment, and supplies

- Prosthetics, orthotics, and prosthetic devices and supplies

- Home health services

- Outpatient prescription drugs

- Inpatient and outpatient hospital services

- Nuclear medicine

These restrictions can also prohibit investment in other businesses that may provide these services. For example, a physician would probably be prohibited from investing in a nursing home or skilled nursing facility if they were ordering lab tests or physical therapy for their patients at the facility.

Whole Hospital Exception & 2010 Ban

For many years, physicians could still invest in "whole hospitals" that may have provided designated health services. The Affordable Care Act of 2010 (ACA) banned the "whole hospital" exception, but also grandfathered in all current physician-owned hospitals in existence before December 31, 2010. The 200 or so physician-owned hospitals in the United States will continue to operate into the foreseeable future, but they may not expand.

ASCs

There is no Stark Law exclusion for ambulatory (outpatient) surgery centers, so surgeons who work at ASCs can invest in them. However, the ASCs are legally required to disclose to their patients that the surgeons are owners in the ASC prior to their surgery.

Rural Exceptions

There is also a rural exception that lets physicians in rural communities (where there is presumably less money) invest in some of the types of businesses prohibited under the Stark Law. The rural exception makes a lot of sense, because physicians are in high demand in rural areas and this investment may augment their income, thereby encouraging them to keep working in rural communities. Rural medical businesses inherently aren't as profitable as urban ones, so whatever benefit physician investors receive would be less than their urban physician counterparts.

In-Office Ancillary Exception

There is an "in-office ancillary" exception to the Stark Law that permits physicians to own and operate services such as x-ray, MRI, physical therapy, labs, ultrasound, and durable medical equipment sales in their offices. These services are considered to be an extension of their practice of medicine. Physician practices are permitted to own these services if all the patient referrals come from inside the group. Physicians from other groups cannot order ancillary services from an ancillary business owned by another physician practice.

Imaging

There is a huge convenience factor for both patients and physicians to be able to receive or perform an x-ray, MRI, or CT scan while the patient is present in the physician's office instead of sending them somewhere else and having to wait to discuss the results at a later time. The Stark Laws only allow physicians in a practice to refer patients to in-office imaging services because the imaging services only serve as an extension of the physician practices.

Laboratory

There are a great number of urinalyses and blood assay tests that can be performed with in-office devices. Many family practices, internal medicine practices, and pediatric practices will purchase such devices so they can get test results instantly rather than add time and administrative burden to the patient evaluation process. The in-office ancillary exception applies directly to in-office lab services.

Physical and Speech Therapy

Under the in-office ancillary exception, orthopedic surgeons may elect to employ physical therapists directly rather than refer their patients to independently practicing therapists, and ear, nose, and throat (ENT) physicians may directly employ speech therapists. There are probably some tangible and intangible benefits to having a formal relationship between orthopedic surgeons and physical therapists as well as ENT physicians and speech therapists. Otherwise, it is conceivable that they may not have any communication during a patient rehabilitation process.

THE ANTI-KICKBACK STATUTE AND THE SAFE HARBORS

The federal Anti-Kickback Statute is a criminal statute that prohibits the payment and receipt of anything of value in an effort to induce or reward the referral of federal healthcare program business.[15] Basically, no one can give a kickback to get patient referrals. This is important because Medicare and Medicaid are federally funded programs and nearly every physician, hospital, and healthcare provider in the United States treats Medicare or Medicaid patients.

The Anti-Kickback Statute is different from the Stark Law. The Stark Law specifically addresses physician referrals to businesses they own. The Anti-Kickback Statute prohibits kickbacks made to any type of healthcare provider that refers patients to another type of healthcare provider, regardless of whether physicians or ownership are involved. So, the Anti-Kickback Statute could apply to a physician referring patients to a hospital as well as a hospital referring patients to a home health agency or nursing home.

Between 1991 and 1999, the government created many safe harbors to the Anti-Kickback Statute. The following list summarizes these safe harbors, though they are too numerous and complicated to explain here.[16]

1. Investment interests in large publicly traded entities or certain small entities

2. Space rentals

3. Equipment rentals

4. Personal services and management contracts

5. Sale of practice

6. Referral services

7. Warranties

8. Discounts

9. Employees

10. Group purchasing organizations

11. Certain Medicare Part A waivers of coinsurance and deductibles

12. Increased coverage, reduced cost-sharing amounts, or reduced premium amounts offered by certain health plans

13. Price reductions offered to certain health plans (managed care)

14. Investment interests in Underserved Areas

15. Investment interests in surgeon-owned single-specialty, multi-specialty and hospital/physician ambulatory surgical centers

16. Investment interests in group practices composed exclusively of active investors who are licensed healthcare professionals

17. Rural practitioner recruitment incentives

18. Obstetrical malpractice insurance subsidies

19. Referral agreements for specialty services

20. Cooperative hospital service organizations

21. Ambulance replenishment arrangements

22. Electronic prescribing and electronic medical records

23. Federally qualified health centers.

So, referral conflicts of interest aside, that leaves several options for physicians and hospitals in terms of joint ventures and buy/sell transactions:

- Surgeons can invest in ASCs.

- Gastroenterologists can invest in endoscopy centers.

- Radiologists can invest in imaging centers.

- Nephrologists can invest in dialysis centers.

- All physicians can invest in real estate and medical office buildings.

- Physicians can own in-office imaging equipment and lab equipment for use in their practices.

- Physicians can employ physical therapists and speech therapists under the in-office ancillary exception.

- Physicians can invest in management companies and clinical co-management companies that manage other medical businesses.

Joint ventures for physician practice ownership are acceptable in some states but not others. In California, for instance, physicians cannot be directly employed by a company or hospital if they are going to practice medicine. In California, physicians can only be employees of physician-owned professional practices and not-for-profit foundations. In other states, though, such as Ohio, anyone can have ownership in a limited liability company (LLC) employing physicians.[17]

A key feature of the exceptions above, including Anti-Kickback Statute safe harbors, Stark Law exceptions, and not-for-profit inurement, is that any investment, sale, purchase, or payment for goods or services rendered must be at Fair Market Value. This is a valuation standard defined as:

> The value at which property would be exchanged between two hypothetical, well-informed parties, when

neither party is compelled to buy or sell, and the parties are not in a position to refer business to each other.

Similarly, while the value of goods or services exchanged may be at a reasonable price, that does not necessarily mean the arrangement is commercially reasonable. Commercial reasonableness basically requires that the arrangement must make business sense, regardless of whether one of the parties is in a position to refer business to the other. In other words, would we still enter into a management services arrangement with this physician group or another management company if these physicians performed no cases at our facility?

JOINT VENTURE GOVERNANCE AND OPERATING AGREEMENT TERMS

The partnership terms of a joint venture's operating agreement are what really align the parties. Operating agreements are legal contracts that dictate the behavior of the owners of a business. The negotiation of operating agreements is a very important task in developing a joint venture because terms set (or not set) at this time will dictate how the owners may act through the life of the business. Terms of operating agreements can include the following:

- **Noncompetes:** The parties may agree to not have ownership interests in competing businesses while they are owners and/or for a period of time after they cease to be owners. This would prohibit both hospitals and physicians from developing and/or investing in competing services. This can also prevent them from competing for several years after they exit the joint venture. Special thought and consideration should be given when considering the geographic radius to which the noncompete applies.

- **Fiduciary duties of the board members:** Representatives on the board of directors have a fiduciary duty to the investors to act in the "best interests" of the joint venture. Even without noncompetes, the board members are still prohibited from investing in competing businesses or being involved in activities that could damage the joint venture financially. This applies to hospital representatives (e.g., CEO, CFO) as well as physicians. Any behavior and actions made by one of the board members that could cause harm to the joint venture is a basis for legal recourse against the offender.

- **Governance and board makeup:** Regular board meetings and subcommittee meetings establish regular, ongoing communication between physician leaders and hospital leadership. Monthly board meetings are usually a good frequency for the first six to eight months of a new joint venture. After that point, board meetings can be quarterly, with a subset of the board meeting monthly to work through management issues.

  More importantly, the operating agreement will establish how the board members are selected, how many hospital representatives and physician representatives will be appointed, term lengths, and whether the board votes their number of seats or ownership percentages. Even if the ownership split is 60% hospital and 40% physicians (or vice versa), the operating agreement may still stipulate that the board of directors have equal representation, with three physicians and three hospital representatives.

- **Board/member/super-majority voting issues:** It is important to establish the decisions that require board approval, approval of the owners, and the level of approval (majority, two-thirds, unanimous) required for each issue.

Generally, board approval should require that neither the hospital nor the physicians can make a decision without some of the members of the other party voting in favor.

Generally speaking, the more important the issue, the more people should be involved in the decision. For example, every owner should have the right to vote on whether or not to sell the business, but the board can make purchase decisions over $10,000 without getting every owner's permission. The process of scheduling a member meeting is extremely difficult when there are more than six owners. Decisions requiring unanimous approval are difficult to pass. That means that just one owner can block an action that all of the other owners support.

The following table presents examples of some business issues and associated levels of approval.

	Board Approval		Member Approval	
Partnership Terms	Majority	75%	Majority	75%
Sell the entire business				X
Buyout of hospital or physicians by the other party				X
Unwind the business and liquidate the assets				X
Annual budget		X		
Purchase decisions over $10,000	X			
Revoke medical privileges of a physician	X			
Transfer of ownership from one physician to another	X			
File legal action on behalf of the joint venture			X	
Approve advertisements or marketing materials	X			
Issue owner distributions	X			
Assume interest bearing long-term debt			X	

- **Ownership transfers/redemptions/sales:** The operating agreement should identify the process and means by which ownership in the joint ventures shall be bought, sold, and valued. There can be serious confrontations over money when these processes are not spelled out in writing.

It is fairly common for an operating agreement to stipulate that a business appraisal be performed periodically to establish the price for ownership interests. Some agreements also establish formulas valuing ownership shares that are explicitly described in the operating agreement.

The original owners need to establish how value will be assessed and what board or member approvals will be necessary for each of the following:

- Sale of ownership from one physician to another

- Sales of ownership from the business to new owners

- Sales of ownership from existing owners to the business

- Transfer of majority ownership from hospital to physicians (or vice versa)

- Redemptions of units for retiring physicians

- Redemptions of units for physicians who pass away

- Redemptions of units for physicians whose medical privileges are revoked

JOINT-VENTURE LIFE CYCLE

While joint ventures can be great mechanisms for aligning physicians and hospitals, they do not last forever. Anecdotally, most joint ventures last between 10 and 15 years. Physician partners retire, the competitive landscape changes, and reimbursement is unpredictable.

Major imaging and surgical equipment as well as building HVAC systems usually need to be replaced every 10 to 12 years. Often the investors in these joint ventures would elect to liquidate with some walk-away money rather than reinvest the business's earnings for two to three years to pay for the replacements.

The parties can benefit financially by planning for the end when the original operating agreement is formulated. The following list identifies several common joint venture dissolution issues that can be prevented by establishing how they will be handled in the original operating agreement.

- If the hospital or physicians are the landlord, will the lease be forgiven in dissolution?

- Will either group (hospital or physicians) have the opportunity to buy the legal business entity (and subsequently be assigned the tax ID, state license, Medicare certification) from the other party?

- Will the equipment be liquidated or will each party have the right to bid on it?

SURGERY CENTERS AND ENDOSCOPY CENTERS

Ambulatory surgery centers or outpatient surgery centers are facilities where patients can have minor surgeries performed and go home the same day of surgery. Patients can usually arrive, have their surgery, and go home within three to four hours. This is a huge benefit over hospital-based surgery, which commonly may be a whole-day affair for the same exact surgeries.

ASCs are generally more efficient because they focus solely on planned elective surgeries, whereas hospitals also provide emergent, unplanned surgeries that sabotage their surgery schedule and cause delays. Additionally, hospitals are large, complex organizations with many more employees, patients, floors, departments, and likelihood of errors. Infection rates tend to be higher in hospitals than ASCs for these reasons.

The most common procedures performed in ASCs are colonoscopies and EGDs, pain injections, orthopedic arthroscopies, and cataract surgery.

Common Outpatient Surgeries by Specialty

Gastro	Pain Management	Ortho	Ophthalmology
Colonoscopy	Epidural Injection	Knee/Shoulder Arthroscopy	Cataract Surgery
EGD	Caudal Injection	Carpel Tunnel Release	Blepharoplasty
General	**Gynecology**	**Urology**	**Plastic**
Hernia	Hysteroscopy	Cystoscopy	Lesion Removal
Gall Bladder	Ablation	Lithotripsy	Breast Augmentation

There are between 5,000 and 6,000 ASCs and endoscopy centers in the United States, and most of them have physician ownership. This is impressive because ASCs weren't even recognized by Medicare until the early 1980s. All of the surgeries and endoscopies that are now performed in ASCs used to be performed in hospitals.

I have observed that there were two quintessential ASC stories in the 1990s.

1. HealthSouth recruited 15 to 25 surgeons from the local hospital to become owners in an ambulatory surgery center joint venture. The hospital administration knew they were going to lose a big chunk of their surgery business, so they formed their own joint ventures with all of the surgeons who did not invest in the HealthSouth deal. This ultimately resulted in two joint ventures in town.

2. The orthopedic surgeons at a hospital heard about a HealthSouth deal and asked the hospital to form an ASC joint venture with them. The hospital CEO said no, and the orthopedic surgeons developed an ASC on their own. A number of surgeons in other specialties followed the orthopedic surgeons. The hospital finally decided to develop their own joint venture with the physicians who were left.

At the time of this writing in 2014, there are more ASCs than there are community hospitals. None of the largest ASC chains (e.g., AmSurg, SCA, or USPI) own more than 5% of the ASCs in the United States, so the market is still heavily fragmented.

While there is definitely a "buy and absorb" strategy by many hospitals, re-absorbing ASC surgeries and billing them under the hospital's payor contracts usually results in a 100% to 300% increase in the price of the surgeries. While this seems like a good business move on the surface, most health plans are structured so the patient bears the first $1,000 to $2,000 of costs as high deductibles as well as 20% to 60% of the remaining costs as coinsurance. In many cases, the majority of the price increases are the burden of the patients.

It is ill-advised for a hospital to acquire an ASC with the sole intent of raising prices on insurance and patients. In fact, ACOs that are reimbursed on a shared savings plan or capitated basis will benefit more financially from low-cost surgery centers than higher prices on fee-for-service business.

IMAGING CENTERS

There are two common ways to align physicians and hospitals with respect to imaging.

Imaging Joint Ventures with Radiologists

Referring physicians are prohibited from investing in imaging centers (except in-office centers), so radiologists are the ideal choice for joint ventures because they do not refer patients. As the physicians who specialize in interpreting imaging tests for MRIs, CTs, mammograms, ultrasounds, and x-rays, radiologists are experts in all things related to imaging.

Outpatient imaging joint ventures are a great way to align a radiology group and a hospital. While the radiologists are still only contractors for inpatient imaging, they truly become owner-partners with the hospital for all outpatient imaging.

Referring back to the governance section, radiologist investment in imaging center joint ventures compels the radiologists to make decisions and act in the best interests of the joint ventures.

The medical imaging business is one of the truly competitive aspects of healthcare in that each imaging center has to compete directly with other imaging centers for patient referrals. Family practice physicians, internists, orthopedists, OBGYNs, pulmonologists, and other specialists have the ability to order imaging tests from multiple imaging centers in their communities. So imaging centers truly do have to provide the best service they can to earn the referrals from physicians.

Imaging centers may spend money on nice finishes to create a "spa" atmosphere, provide patients with soft robes or warm blankets while they are being scanned, or play music for patients during their scan.

Imaging centers, unlike many other medical businesses, may employ dedicated marketing employees to visit referring physician practices to meet with referrers, provide education, or get friendly with office staff who schedule imaging testing for patients.

Purchasing In-Office Imaging Centers from Physicians

Another way to align physicians and hospitals is for hospitals to purchase the in-office imaging services from physicians. A few examples:

1.   An orthopedic group can sell their in-office MRI business to the hospital. The group signs a three-year noncompete

with the sale and the hospital continues to operate the MRI imaging business.

2. An OBGYN group sells their in-office ultrasound business to the hospital.

3. A cardiology group sells their in-office echo ultrasound business to the hospital.

4. An internal medicine practice sells their in-office CT scanner to the hospital.

The sale of in-office ancillary services will usually involve a significant amount of financial risk for the buyer, and subsequently they are risky businesses to purchase. This is because there is nothing the buyer can do to prevent physicians from referring their patients to another imaging center. A noncompete only prevents the seller from recreating another in-office imaging center. There is nothing the buyer can legally do to make physicians refer patients to the newly acquired imaging business.

Similarly, the physicians could sell their practice to a competing hospital and be physically relocated. There is absolutely nothing the purchaser of the ancillary services can do to prevent the physician practice from moving.

SPECIALTY/SURGICAL HOSPITALS

The ACA banned physician ownership in surgical hospitals and specialty hospitals, with a grandfather clause for the 200 or so existing ones. The existing surgical hospitals have restrictions on ownership that prevent them from increasing physician ownership in the future. This creates a number of partnership opportunities.

Surgical hospitals are major investments from a real estate and improvement standpoint. It is not uncommon for surgical facility construction costs to be $300 per square foot or more just for the improvements. This does not include the core and shell costs for the foundation and walls. Because so much money is invested to comply with the state, federal, and accrediting organization regulations for surgical facilities, there is very little chance that these buildings can be repurposed for anything other than performing surgeries.

Because future physician investment in surgical hospitals is prohibited, the pool of potential buyers is limited to other local hospitals, public hospital chains, and lay people. The number of physician-owned hospitals will decrease as more time passes because the pool of physician investors can only shrink. The specialty heart hospital business MedCath liquidated in 2012, and National Surgical Hospitals sold out to a private equity firm.

DIALYSIS/VASCULAR ACCESS CENTERS

Ongoing renal dialysis for patients in kidney failure is a relatively low-cost service to provide. The dialysis companies I've spoken to say that they can develop a dialysis center around the practice of a single nephrologist. This is significantly easier than surgery centers and cath labs that may require 10 to 15 surgeons or more to generate enough volume to turn a profit. Dialysis is not a designated health service under the Stark Laws.

The publicly traded companies DaVita and Fresenius collectively account for about 60% of the dialysis centers in the United States. Their market share is so complete in the United States that most of their future growth, if any, will likely have to come from abroad.

Dialysis centers are comprised of relatively cheap office space with recliners and infusion equipment for dialysis patients. The patients sit and watch television while their blood is intravenously removed, cleansed, and pumped back into their bodies. The procedure itself is relatively low risk, but it has to be done at least three to four hours per day, three times per week, for the rest of their lives. Medicare, the primary payor for dialysis, traditionally pays for treatment three times per week. Patients who self-fund dialysis for themselves every day or pay to have dialysis performed in their homes often report feeling much better than those who only get treated the minimum.

Another medical service that is closely related to dialysis is provided by vascular access centers (VACs). Vascular access, as it relates to dialysis, is the installment of venous catheters and the creation of fistulas for dialysis purposes. If you need dialysis, you can get a catheter installed as a short-term solution, but they will probably need to create a fistula or graft for long-term access. Fistulas and grafts are created by connecting a vein to an artery to make a strong, large access point where lots of blood flow will occur.

These procedures can be performed in a physician's office or in a dedicated facility such as a surgery center or a hospital department. Both interventional radiologists and nephrologists with interventional training can perform these procedures.

MANAGEMENT AND CO-MANAGEMENT WITH PHYSICIANS

When physicians are bought out of a surgery center or surgical hospital, they lose their vested interest, as is the case with any divested business owner. It is commonplace for an acquirer to engage the divested former owner as a consultant or keep them on in some sort of contractual management arrangement. A key feature of management and co-management arrangements is that the contractor is locked into a restrictive noncompete clause.

Management agreements and co-management agreements are standard arrangements with respect to surgical hospitals. More information on these agreements is presented in the next chapter.

CARDIAC CATHETERIZATION LABS

With adequate pre-operative screening, diagnostic catheterizations of heart disease patients and post-surgical transplant patients can be safely performed in outpatient cath labs. It is fairly common for hospitals and cardiologists to form cath lab joint ventures and perform these outpatient procedures in a facility that is physically separate from the hospital but still in close proximity. Though Medicare does cover cardiac catheterization performed in freestanding facilities that are not wholly hospital-owned, there are still some states that do not permit freestanding catheterization labs or joint ventures. An assessment by the Agency for Healthcare Research and Quality (AHRQ) found that 13 states have regulations specifically prohibiting cardiac catheterization in freestanding clinics.[18]

Like ASCs, cath lab joint ventures are as much a defensive move as they are joint ventures. The hospital would rather share 50% (or more) of their facility fee with the cardiologists than risk the chance that they could lose 100% of the cardiologists' cases when a competing hospital or other third party partners with the cardiologists to form a competing cardiac cath lab.

Heart diseases such as congestive heart failure, hypertension, coronary artery disease, atrial fibrillation, heart attacks, cardiomyopathy, and cardiomegaly are big business for hospitals that provide such cardiology services as cath labs, balloon angioplasty, atherectomy, nuclear imaging, ECHO cardiograms, bypass graft surgery, and Da Vinci robot surgery. The equipment purchases associated with these services are costly.

When a competing hospital creates a joint venture with cardiologists for a cath lab, it may make it more convenient for the cardiologists to perform other types of procedures at the competing hospital as well. For example, if Dr. Smith has block schedule times at the cath lab joint venture every Monday and

Wednesday morning, it may be more convenient for him or her to have block surgery times those same afternoons rather than drive back across town and lose 30 to 45 minutes or otherwise productive clinical time in travel.

Conversely, with any joint venture it is important to verify the financial feasibility of the venture before investments are made. Cardiologists may not keep an accurate count of how many catheterizations they are performing on a regular basis. I've had dozens of surgeons tell me he or she performed hundreds of cases per year and later find out he or she only averaged less than half as many as they thought.

Volume projections have to be airtight. Business development executives should get data downloads or reports from each physician's practice management system and verify those against whatever volumes are being performed at known hospitals. Cannibalizing the partner hospital department's cases is a tough nut for CFOs to swallow, but I can't tell you how many times I've seen surgeons pull 100% of their cases out of a hospital because the administration blew off their request to form a joint venture partnership.

RADIATION THERAPY CENTERS

Family practice and internal medicine physicians often refer cancer patients to *medical* oncologists. If medical treatment via chemotherapy is deemed unsuccessful or likely to be unsuccessful, the medical oncologists may refer their patients to specialists in surgery or radiation oncology.

Radiation oncologists oversee the administration of radiation therapy that is directly administered by a radiation physicist, dosimetrist, and therapist with a linear accelerator. Linear accelerators are major medical equipment devices used in radiation therapy centers.

Radiation therapy centers can be owned by radiation oncologists through the in-office Stark exception. However, unlike ASCs, which are not a designated health service under Stark, radiation therapy centers cannot be joint ventured with physicians and hospitals, health systems, or chain operators. Physicians can only own a radiation therapy center if it is an *extension of their own practice.*

Therefore, a hospital or other organization can purchase a radiation oncology center from an oncology practice, but the hospital cannot force the oncologists to refer patients for treatment to the center. As with ASCs, the buyer is reliant on noncompete clauses in the purchase agreement, medical directorships, clinical co-management arrangements, and real estate leases to maintain alignment with the physicians.

Chapter 4
Contract Deals

OVERVIEW

This chapter discusses the following topics related to contractual service business arrangements with physicians:

- Basic Elements of Contractual Service Arrangements

- Fraud and Abuse Allegations at Columbia/HCA

- Fraud and Abuse Allegations at Tenet Healthcare

- On-Call Physician Coverage and Compensation

- Stipends, Subsidies, and Collections Guarantees for Hospital–Based Specialty Coverage

- Professional Interpretation Services

- Anesthesiology Coverage Contract

- Medical Directorships

- Professional Management and Co-Management

- Clinical Services PSAs

- Gainsharing

- Nonclinical Arrangements

BASIC ELEMENTS OF CONTRACTUAL SERVICE ARRANGEMENTS

Most doctor deals can be classified into one of two categories: joint ventures or contractual service arrangements.

In joint ventures, the physicians and hospitals each invest their own money in business ventures together. If the joint ventures are successful, both parties benefit, but if the joint ventures flounder or fail, both parties are subject to possible investment losses and associated financial risks. The parties are mutually aligned and incentivized by the joint venture's ability to succeed.

In contractual service arrangements, physicians and hospitals buy and sell legitimate services from each other. In contractual arrangements, there is less investment risk and less potential reward involved. For example, a radiologist providing medical director services to an imaging center is not compensated any more or less if the imaging center is financially successful or not. However, a radiologist who is an investor in an imaging center joint venture shares in the center's financial success or failure.

Legitimate professional service arrangements between physicians and hospitals or other medical facilities should include several elements. At a very basic level, every arrangement should minimally include:

1. A written legal agreement drafted by an attorney with healthcare experience stating the services to be provided and the compensation amount.

2. A Fair Market Value analysis to determine appropriate pricing for the services.

3. Some mechanism to verify that the physician and/or other party are actually providing the services. For example, most medical director agreements require the physician

to keep logs of the time spent performing the services.

These are not just rules of thumb. Fraud and abuse cases brought by the Office of the Inspector General (OIG) (the fraud division of the Department of Health and Human Services), the Justice Department, and the IRS examine these three items, among others, when they investigate an arrangement. A qualified and experienced healthcare attorney will rely on these and other tests to establish compliance under the safe harbors for the Anti-Kickback Statute and the Stark Law exceptions.

FRAUD AND ABUSE ALLEGATIONS AT COLUMBIA/HCA

In 1968, Dr. Thomas Frist, Sr., Jack C. Massey and Dr. Thomas Frist, Jr. formed a hospital management company to manage Park View Hospital in Nashville, Tennessee. The company, Hospital Corporation of America (HCA), grew to operate 11 hospitals and filed for initial public offering in 1969. In the 1980s HCA acquired General Care Corporation, General Health Services, Hospital Affiliates International, and Health Care Corporation. By 1987 the company operated 463 hospitals (255 owned and 208 managed). In 1994 HCA merged with Columbia. Columbia/HCA operated over 350 hospitals, 145 outpatient surgery centers, and 550 home care agencies.[19] Columbia's founder, Richard Scott, an attorney, became CEO of the combined companies.

Over 30 whistle-blowers filed complaints against Columbia/HCA with the government between 1993 and 1997, including Jim Alderson, who had been dismissed as CFO of the Quorum facility (an HCA spin-off) North Valley Hospital in Whitefish, Montana in 1990.[20] Another whistle-blower, certified public accountant John Schilling, also came forward to regulators in 2006 and agreed to wear a wire while returning to Columbia/HCA as a consultant in 2007. Schilling recounted his involvement in his book *Undercover: How I Went from Company Man to FBI Spy and Exposed the Worst Healthcare Fraud in U.S. History.*

Columbia/HCA engaged in many different fraudulent acts to which the company ultimately pled guilty. Many of the acts were related to upcoding and fraudulent billing practices as well as fraudulent Medicare cost report accounting. Though fraudulent billing and accounting practices represented the bulk of the improprieties, systemic patterns of physician kickbacks were also revealed.

James Thompson, now a retired physician, was another whistle-blower against Columbia/HCA. Thompson ultimately received $41 million as a reward from the federal government for his involvement in the case.

Thompson notified the FBI that he and many doctors received ownership shares in Columbia hospitals without investing any money. The Justice Department lawyers said the company matched these "sham investments" to the patient referrals received from physicians. These were clear violations of the kickback laws because Columbia was giving physicians valuable company stock as rewards for patient referrals.

Thompson told a newspaper, "All of the shares I got, I never paid a dime for."[21] According to the legal complaint filed in Texas, HCA gave physicians loans without the expectation of repayment, free rent, free office remodeling, and free drugs from hospital pharmacies that could be resold by physicians.[22]

In mid-March 1997, investigators from the FBI, the Internal Revenue Service, and the Department of Health and Human Services served search warrants on Columbia facilities in El Paso as well as dozens of physician offices.[23] Over the next six years, Columbia/HCA would be investigated by the Department of Justice, the FBI, the OIG, and dozens of district attorneys in several states.[24]

CEO Richard Scott resigned his position in July 1997, a week after law enforcement agents raided 35 Columbia offices in seven states.[25] Scott received over $5.0 million in cash, $300 million in stock options, and a five year consulting job with HCA worth $950,000 annually.[26,27] Scott was never interviewed by government officials or charged with any wrongdoing.

A Columbia/HCA board member engaged attorney Jerre Frazier to evaluate the company's problems. Frazier was cited in the *Tampa Bay Times* as saying he did not believe Scott personally approved any illegal conduct, but he believed Rick was aware of the company's conduct and that he had warned Scott.[21] Frazier was hired on as a compliance officer for HCA in 1997 and stayed through 1999. Frazier would later become a whistle-blower in a 2005 case alleging that IASIS Healthcare paid phony medical directorships to physicians and offered physicians office space at less than fair market value.[28]

Dr. Frist, Jr. returned as Chairman and CEO of HCA after Scott's departure and instituted restructuring. In May 1999, HCA completed the spin-off of LifePoint and Triad Hospitals.

In December 2000, HCA entered into a settlement with the Department of Justice to pay $840 million to settle criminal claims against the company.[24] As part of the settlement, HCA entered into an eight-year corporate integrity agreement with the Office of the Inspector General of the Department of Health and Human Services imposing significant compliance requirements on the company.[29] In June 2003, HCA would also agree to settle its civil claims for an additional $881 million. Within the 2003 settlement, $620 million was related to settling eight whistle-blower lawsuits, of which $225.5 million was specifically related to the payment of kickbacks and other illegal compensation paid to physicians for patient referrals.[30] The combined total settlement was $1.7 billion. At the time, this was by far the largest recovery ever made by the government for a healthcare fraud investigation.

According to various sources, HCA and Quorum's combined legal defense cost $300 million compared to the $20 million to $30 million budget the federal government dedicated.[20,28]

In November 2006, HCA was taken private in a $33 billion transaction that was the largest leveraged buyout in history at the time. HCA became a publicly traded company once again in March 2011.

HCA currently operates 165 hospitals and 115 freestanding surgery centers in 20 states and England, and employs about 204,000 people. HCA estimates that it provides four to five percent of all inpatient care delivered in the United States.[31]

HCA's former CEO, Richard Scott, was elected governor of Florida in 2011 and will run for reelection in 2014.

John Ford, the lead investigator in the Columbia/HCA case, would later lead the Enron investigation and eventually be promoted to Assistant Director of the FBI. Ford was quoted in Schilling's book as saying that he regretted that the government did not pursue individuals for criminal charges on the Columbia/HCA case.[28]

It was not until after Columbia/HCA that Ford realized that individual corporate officers had to be held accountable, rather than just imposing financial penalties on their companies. Ford pointed out that after the Columbia/HCA case, the government did a better job of focusing on pursuing corporate executives for criminal charges. Acknowledging his mistake with Columbia/HCA, Ford indicated that they deliberately pursued prison sentences for corporate executives in subsequent cases with Enron, Qwest, WorldCom, and HealthSouth.

FRAUD AND ABUSE ALLEGATIONS AT TENET HEALTHCARE

While Columbia/HCA was the largest for-profit hospital chain during the 1990s and early 2000s, Tenet Healthcare (Tenet) was the second-largest hospital chain. Tenet had several bad experiences with physician kickbacks. In fact, Tenet was originally named National Medical Enterprises (NME). It changed its name after a particularly bad scandal with psychiatric hospitals, during which many healthy patients were admitted to psychiatric institutions and held against their will to maximize insurance payments. In 1994, NME pled guilty to over a half dozen criminal charges, including paying kickbacks and bribes to physicians for referring and admitting patients to their hospitals. NME paid $379 million to the government related to the charges[32] and would eventually pay over $750 million by the time all settlements with health insurance companies and patients were finished. Over a half dozen individuals, including four psychiatrists, were criminally convicted. The longest prison sentence handed down was eight years.

The financial pressure imposed on publicly traded companies to maximize shareholder stock value is immense. Only a few years after the NME psychiatric hospital scandal, new scandals at two Tenet hospitals in California were exposed. This kicked off years of government investigations and trials resulting in over $1.0 billion dollars in new settlements between 2003 and 2006.

Redding Medical Center

Throughout the 1990s and early 2000s, Redding Medical Center in Redding, California, was a financial gem in Tenet's hospital network. According to a 4,000-word exposé in *The New York Times* in 2003, the California Heart Institute at Redding Medical Center was bursting at the seams in the winter of 1998.[33] That year, Redding Medical Center exceeded its budget for pretax profit by almost 50 percent, netting $50 million. Despite stellar performance, Tenet's management budgeted for additional growth at RMC the following year.

The secret of RMC's financial breakout was two physicians: Dr. Chae Hyun Moon, the chief cardiologist, and Dr. Fidel Realyvasquez, a cardiac surgeon. Dr. Moon was notorious for aggressively ordering cardiac catheterizations and referring patients to surgeon Dr. Realyvasquez for coronary artery bypass grafts (CABGs). During the twelve months ending in June 2002, Dr. Moon performed 876 cardiac catheterizations for the left side of the heart. During his tenure at RMC, Moon performed over 35,000 catherizations.[33] The 1999 Dartmouth Atlas of Health Care reported that RMC had the highest bypass surgery rate in the United States in 1995 and 1996. It would later be revealed that Dr. Realyvasquez performed a triple bypass on a twenty-eight-year-old as well as numerous other patients regarded as not needing open heart surgery by other cardiologists. In 2004, 769 patients would file legal claims against Moon, Realyvasquez, and Tenet.

During the 1990s, RMC was host to seven different hospital CEOs. Numerous community physicians notified RMC's CEOs of their concerns about Moon's and Realyvasquez's aggressive treatments. Unlike other hospitals, which relied on peer review of physician performance, RMC's peer review for cardiology was led by Dr. Moon himself. No third-party peer reviews were ever commissioned, or if any were, they were never made public.

According to Stephen Klaidman's book recounting the scandal, *CORONARY: A True Story of Medicine Gone Awry*, despite being independent contractors, both Dr. Moon and Dr. Realyvasquez received excessive compensation from RMC to incentivize them to refer patients for services. Klaidman's book indicates that Dr. Realyvasquez demanded over one million dollars per year from

RMC for nine to ten years. Allegedly, Dr. Moon received $120,000 per year for his medical director services, while Dr. Realyvasquez received $180,000 per year for his medical director services. Both Moon and Realyvasquez were compensated through a variety of devices, including their medical directorships, salaries and bonuses, emergency-call pay, subsidies for practice expenses and staff, and the provision of aircraft for physician use.

Over the years, numerous whistle-blowers came forward to the FBI and the California Medical Board, including patients, physicians, lawyers, and even a Catholic priest. Finally, on October 30, 2002, 42 federal officials raided RMC and Moon's and Realyvasquez's offices.[34] The team, led by FBI agent Mike Skeen, included agents from the Internal Revenue Service, Drug Enforcement Agency, Medicare fraud specialists from the Department of Health and Human Services (DHHS), FBI computer specialists, and a dozen support staff members. The local police chief had to excuse himself from participating because his wife was an administrator at RMC.

The Department of Justice's case ultimately proved to be too difficult to pursue criminally, for which the standard of proof is *beyond a reasonable doubt*. Prosecutors feared a case required to define medical standards of care would turn into an indecisive battle of experts. The standard of proof for civil cases is only a *preponderance of evidence*. So while neither Moon, nor Realyvasquez would ever see prison, the maximum payout under their malpractice policies would likely prohibit them from ever acquiring malpractice coverage again. Not being able to get malpractice coverage would become a major impediment to Moon's and Realyvasquez's ability to practice medicine. The Department of Justice ultimately fined Moon and Realyvasquez $1.4 million each.[35] Moon's and Realyvasquez's malpractice insurance policies collectively maxed out for $24 million in settlements.

Tenet settled its portion of the government's case for $54 million in 2003. While Tenet was also not prosecuted on criminal charges, RMC was still at risk of being excluded from the Medicare program by DHHS. Tenet subsequently sold the hospital to another operator.

While Moon and Realyvasquez were allegedly the individuals actually providing unnecessary medical services, Tenet ended up paying over ten times as much money as the physicians, purely because it had deeper pockets. Tenet settled a suit brought by the 769 patients for $395 million.

Alvarado Hospital

FBI agents raided Tenet's Alvarado Hospital in San Diego in December 2002. Alvarado's CEO was charged in June 2003 and Alvarado's associate administrator and business development executive was charged in September 2003 with paying illegal kickbacks of $10 million under the guise of "sham" relocation expenses for four physicians.[36]

Evidently, Alvarado Hospital was a test for the government, because it subsequently subpoenaed documents from many more Tenet facilities.

- April 17, 2003: The Office of the Inspector General (OIG) of DHHS subpoenaed documents related to agreements with physicians affiliated with five Tenet hospitals in California and Nevada.[37]

- July 2003: Federal prosecutors subpoenaed physician-recruitment records at all of Tenet's 114 hospitals, and the United States Attorney's Office in Los Angeles sought detailed information about seven of Tenet's southern California hospitals.[38]

- August 2003: Florida state officials subpoenaed employee

and physician contracts dating back to 1992, including loans and purchase and sale agreements.[39]

- March 2004: The Justice Department asked Tenet to submit documents related to financial relationships between two El Paso hospitals and 23 physicians in two groups.[40]

- October 2004: A physician interviewed in TheStreet.com claimed Tenet's Century City Hospital in California paid "totally phony" directorships to his competitors in exchange for patient referrals.[41] One physician at a North Ridge Medical Center in Florida was paid $25,000 for a medical directorship that the previous physician filled for no compensation, while another physician was compensated for being the international marketing director for promoting the hospital's services in the Caribbean islands.

If successful, the case against Alvarado Hospital case was likely to be the model for the rest of United States Attorneys to follow for sham relocation payments and sham medical directorships. However, the trial proved fairly difficult. Because the laws were complicated and difficult to understand, there were two mistrials resulting in hung juries. The government ultimately gave up and settled during the third trial. Proceedings began in October 2004 and extended until May 2006, when Tenet agreed to pay a relatively small $21 million civil settlement.[42] Tenet also agreed to either sell Alvarado Hospital or have it be excluded from the Medicare program.

One month later, in June 2006, the DOJ announced that Tenet subsequently entered into a $900 million settlement related to alleged unlawful billing practices nationwide.[43] Within the $900 million settlement, $47 million was specifically related to resolving claims that Tenet paid kickbacks to physicians.

ON-CALL PHYSICIAN COVERAGE AND COMPENSATION

In order to operate a hospital you need physicians from a variety of specialties to be available at all times to provide consultations and treat patients in the emergency department, inpatient unit, intensive care unit, pediatric inpatient unit, and obstetrics. It used to be a requirement that if you were a credentialed physician on the medical staff of the hospital, you had to take "call," meaning that you had to be available several days a month to take phone calls for full 24 hour periods and go into the hospital if needed. Call coverage was provided by the physicians at no cost. They had to do it if they wanted privileges to treat their patients at the hospital.

A few years back, hospitals started paying for on-call coverage availability. The rates paid for on-call coverage are a fraction of what the physicians make on an hourly basis. The physicians can be paid for a 24-hour shift or a shorter or longer period of time.

The federal statute EMTALA (Emergency Medical Treatment and Active Labor Act) actually requires hospitals to establish a list of on-call physicians who can be reached when they are needed. Generally speaking, if a hospital provides inpatient services that may need to be rendered on an emergent basis, they need to establish an arrangement with physicians to provide those services on a 24/7/365 basis.[44] Additionally, some states specifically set staffing requirements requiring physicians or other medical providers to be on-site for particular service lines. For instance, California Children's Services requires board-certified pediatric intensivists to be on-site for intensive care unit coverage 24/7.[45]

Restricted call coverage is defined as on-site coverage. Specialties like emergency medicine, pediatric intensive care, intensive care/critical care, and hospitalist medicine are typically required to provide continuous on-site coverage 24/7/365. Obviously, a single physician cannot provide more than a few days of on-site coverage per month, so hospitals may have a call panel of four to 20 (or more) specialists who rotate on-site call. The hospital may even provide a room where physicians can sleep while on call.

Unrestricted call coverage is defined as off-site coverage. Off-site call coverage is how hospitals procure availability for specialist consults for their emergency room. A patient with a broken bone (orthopedic) or appendicitis (general surgery) could walk into the emergency department at any time. However, these incidents can be few and far between. Hospitals usually can't afford to hire physician specialists to provide on-site call for their emergency departments. The physicians just don't see enough patients to justify their time and expense. Therefore, hospitals let the physicians provide the coverage remotely. The physicians are called to determine if they need to come in to the emergency department on a case-by-case basis.

The following table identifies hospital departments and the related medical specialists that may provide call coverage.

Department	Restricted Call	Unrestricted Call
Emergency Department	Emergency Medicine	Orthopedic Surgeons
		General Surgeons
		Cardiologists
		Ophthalmology
		Neurologists
		OBGYNs
Inpatient Unit	Hospitalists	Family Medicine
		Internal Medicine
Pediatric Unit	Pediatricians	
Intensive Care Unit (ICU)	Critical Care	
	Intensivists	
Pediatric Intensive Care (PICU)	Pediatric Intensivists	
Neonatology	Neonatologists	
Labor and Delivery		OBGYNs

The terms call coverage, on-call coverage, and professional coverage are sometimes used interchangeably by hospital counsel and hospital administrators. On-call coverage is generally associated with securing physician availability, whether on-site or off-site.

All previous factors considered, call coverage is not always compensated. The economics of certain markets and types of coverage arrangements may not present the need for compensation.

In some situations, where the economic factors are favorable, or there are physician groups competing for an exclusive coverage arrangement, physicians may enter into call arrangements or coverage arrangements with no hospital compensation component. For example, if General Hospital has the ability to contract with two different neonatology groups for NICU coverage as well as a national provider like Pediatrix, and the volume and payor mix for the NICU is adequate to support a desirable level of physician compensation, then all three groups may propose to provide the coverage with no supplemental compensation to keep their offers competitive.

Similarly, if there are two anesthesiology groups in town, one of them may propose to provide anesthesiology coverage of the hospital's surgical program without hospital compensation because they are trying to create a competitive advantage that the other group may not be able to offer.

Taking call can also be a great way for specialists to build referrals. Some of the busiest surgeons I have ever met were taking call at several hospitals in large cities just to get the patient referrals. This is because the patients that each physician is called to treat will typically become their patient when they respond. What's even better is that many call events do not require the physician to appear on-site. For example, a patient who tears their rotator cuff or ligaments in their knees can be sent home from the emergency department with instructions to go to the orthopedic surgeon's office on Monday. This creates new patients for a surgeon who just had to take a brief phone call to get them.

Daily on-call compensation rates can vary widely depending on the frequency at which the physicians are called and the frequency of their need to physically go to the hospital. Off-site on-call rates might be as low as $35 per day for physician specialties that are not called often to well over $1,500 per day for specialists who are called often or in specialties with very limited demand.

In some parts of the country, particularly rural and remote areas, there are not enough physicians available to provide all of the call coverage that hospitals need. For example, I recently read about a general surgeon in Eureka, California, who provided 150 days of consecutive call coverage.[46]

STIPENDS, SUBSIDIES, AND COLLECTIONS GUARANTEES FOR HOSPITAL-BASED SPECIALTY COVERAGE

Hospitals may utilize practice subsidies or collections guarantees to compensate independent physician groups that provide exclusive 24/7 coverage of a hospital service line. Some of the most popular physician specialists to receive subsidies and collection guarantees practice in hospital-based specialties such as anesthesiology, radiology, emergency medicine, hospitalist medicine, neonatology, critical care, pediatric critical care, and pediatric hospital medicine. These types of specialists work primarily in hospital or facility settings and may be required to provide on-site coverage 24 hours per day.

If there are not enough patients to keep the physicians busy, or if they treat a high proportion of Medicaid, Medicare, or self-pay patients, the physicians may not collect enough fees to adequately support themselves financially. When coverage is required, but professional collections are not adequate enough to support the physicians, hospitals and physicians will enter into financial support payment arrangements.

Collections guarantees usually involve monthly payments to the physician practice with a periodic reconciliation to make sure the physicians are not making too much money. If the practice is overpaid, there may be a payback mechanism or credit applied against future payments. Practice subsidies also involve monthly payments, but the payment amount is usually fixed with no reconciliation.

Collections guarantees and subsidies are different from call coverage in several respects. First, on call is really just compensation for two specific things. This includes payment of physician availability and possible compensation for patients they treat who may not have the ability to pay. Recall that on-call arrangements are typically for 24-hour periods of availability. A single physician group may only account for 25% of the total on-call coverage that is provided for a particular specialty. In this respect, on-call compensation is compartmentalized.

Second, collections guarantees and subsidies are usually for comprehensive, exclusive coverage of a particular hospital department, such as 24/7/365 coverage of the emergency department by a single group or 24/7/365 coverage of the operating rooms by an anesthesiology group. In this respect, collections guarantees and subsidies are usually restricted to one group's complete coverage of a particular hospital department.

Third, collections guarantees and subsidies are inclusive of on-call coverage. This means that if Pediatric Specialists Group is contracted to provide 24/7/365 coverage of the pediatric unit, including both 24/7/365 on-site coverage and on-call backup coverage, and General Hospital guarantees they will collect a set amount of collections for all those services provided, that collections guarantee includes the practice's cost to provide on-call coverage. Alternatively, General Hospital could pay on-call coverage separately.

To establish if a collection guarantee or subsidy is warranted, an FMV assessment needs to be performed to establish appropriate compensation.

For example, suppose it is determined that Anesthesiology Consultants must employ 12 anesthesiologists to provide the necessary surgical and ER coverage that Memorial Medical Center needs.

The staffing requirements include multiple anesthesiologists on-site during daytime operating hours, one physician on-site during the evening, and backup anesthesiologists on call during evenings. For illustrative purposes, let's suppose that it was determined that the cost associated with staffing 12 anesthesiologists is $5,400,000. This cost includes salaries, benefits, and practice overhead costs.

Anesthesiology Consultants provides collections reports indicating that its professional collections for services provided at Memorial Medical Center are $4.2 million per year. Therefore, the implied shortfall is $1.2 million ($5.4 million for the services less $4.2 million of collections). Therefore, there is sufficient evidence to support an annual subsidy payment of $1.2 million (normally divided among equal monthly payments) or a collections guarantee of $5.4 million (the cost to provide the services).

Collections guarantees and subsidies are commonly used to subsidize physician coverage for several hospital departments, including those shown in the following table.

Department	Specialty
Emergency Department	Emergency Medicine
Inpatient Med/Surg Unit	Hospitalists
Imaging	Radiologists
Surgery	Anesthesiology
Pediatric Unit	Pediatricians
Intensive Care Unit (ICU)	Critical Care Physicians
	Intensivists
Pediatric Intensive Care (PICU)	Pediatric Intensivists
Neonatology (NICU)	Neonatologists
Labor and Delivery	Obstetric-Gynecologists (OBGYN)

In the preceding table you will notice many of the same departments and physician specialties that were identified in the on-call section of this chapter.

There are major inner-city hospitals as well as rural hospitals that have very poor payor mixes, meaning that a high proportion of their patients are covered under Medicaid or they are simply uninsured and have very limited ability to afford medical care. Many hospitals are subsidizing physician coverage for half a dozen or more of their departments, and some of these subsidies are millions of dollars each.

Even so, there are many physician groups that provide 24/7/365 coverage with no subsidization. In fact, some hospitals are in a position wherein several physician groups may competitively bid for an exclusive coverage contract because they want the business. There are several national physician staffing and management companies, including IPC: The Hospitalist Company, Pediatrix, and Surgical Affiliates Management Group, which will recruit and create physician practices exclusively to provide coverage to hospital departments.

PROFESSIONAL INTERPRETATION SERVICES

Professional interpretation is obviously most common among radiologists and pathologists, but there are also large markets for cardiologists to read echocardiograms and for primary care physicians or critical care physicians to read EKGs.

While a hospital or imaging center usually owns the diagnostic equipment (e.g., an MRI, CT, x-ray, ultrasound, DEXA scanner) and employs specially trained technologists to operate the machines, only radiologists are technically trained to interpret the results of such devices. Therefore, usually two claims are generated for a diagnostic test—the technical services provided by the facility and the professional service provided by the radiologist.

Again, because corporations cannot traditionally employ physicians (though this is starting to change), imaging centers typically engage in professional interpretation agreements with physicians to provide these services. In exchange for an exclusive interpretation arrangement, radiologists enter into these agreements with specifically identified terms for who will provide the interpretations, how quickly they will turn around the interpretations, and their hours of availability.

Radiology is somewhat unique from other physician specialties because radiology interpretations can be provided from almost anywhere. MRIs and other scanned images can be transferred electronically and interpreted from great distances away. This gives radiologists great flexibility in their ability to stay productive. A radiologist sitting in a remote office can continuously read imaging studies all day as they come in from multiple facilities.

For this and other reasons, radiologists may or may not need collections guarantees or subsidies to support their coverage, unless the payor mix is very poor or their interpretation agreement restricts them to only read for a single facility during coverage hours. Such restrictions affect a radiologist's ability to be billable and productive.

ANESTHESIOLOGY COVERAGE CONTRACT

Anesthesiology for surgery, labor and delivery, the emergency department, and pain management is usually provided at each hospital by a single anesthesiology physician group through an exclusive contract. Hospitals engage a single group to exclusively meet all their anesthesiology needs because this ensures consistency when the same anesthesiologists are present day after day. It is undesirable to have new anesthesiologists rotating in and out all the time.

It is the author's opinion that the leader of the anesthesiology group is one of the most important physicians in the hospital. The anesthesiologists are present for every surgery with every surgeon and every delivery with every OBGYN. They also consult for the emergency physicians in the ED and the internists and hospitalists in the inpatient unit. No other physicians are regularly interacting with so many other types of physicians on an ongoing daily basis. Most other types of physicians work in silos. They rarely get face time with their peers. Certainly no one gets as much face time with so many other physicians as anesthesiologists do.

As a result, anesthesiologists, as a group, tend to have more firsthand knowledge about what is going on with their peers than anyone else. They have great intelligence on some of the most vital hospital service lines: surgery, labor and delivery, emergency services, and the inpatient floor.

MEDICAL DIRECTORSHIPS

Physicians may be retained to perform nonclinical, administrative services for hospitals, long-term care facilities, post-acute rehab facilities, surgery centers, imaging centers, home health agencies, dialysis centers, and other types of medical organizations. Outpatient medical businesses usually operate under the Drug Enforcement Agency (DEA) license of the medical director (ASCs, imaging centers, etc.).

Depending on the size of the business, the medical director may spend one to 40 hours per week providing administrative services. Most medical directorships are part-time in nature. Physicians serving as medical directors frequently have their own full-time practices and provide medical director services on the side. For example, it is common for internal medicine physicians to serve as medical directors of one or more nursing homes.

There is a legitimate need for medical directorships because many medical businesses would otherwise not have any medically licensed oversight. For example, imaging centers have technologists who operate the machines and serve as managers and supervisors, but without medical directors, they would go for extended periods of time without ever having a physician on-site. Fortunately, imaging centers engage medical directors so they have physicians involved in operations, even if is just for a few hours a week.

Medical directors should specialize in a discipline that is directly related to the facility or business they oversee. Radiologists oversee imaging centers, anesthesiologists oversee surgery centers, nephrologists oversee dialysis centers, and internists oversee nursing homes.

Medical directorships are extremely common in healthcare. Every ambulatory surgery center (>5,000), independent diagnostic imaging center (>6,000), post-acute home health agency (>10,000), and nursing home (>15,000) has at least one medical director. Within hospitals (~5,500) you will have several medical directors for the various clinical areas that can include the ICU, NICU, pediatrics, PICU, hospitalist medicine, radiology, anesthesiology, endoscopy, pathology, and a variety of other departments.

Oversight is a pretty common duty in medical directorship agreements, and unfortunately it is a duty that can be difficult to measure. I've seen several medical directorships wherein the physicians were actually being paid to do very little. While it is illegal to give physicians money for services they are not actually performing, at the same time it is very difficult to prove someone is or is not providing oversight.

When picking the duties to go into a medical directorship agreement, I recommend getting out the job descriptions for the business's administrator, director of nursing, and other managers and making sure there are no redundancies. Many medical director agreements identify duties that are commonly performed by the business's managers.

For example, I have seen medical director agreements that state that the medical director is responsible for the business's TJC accreditation. However, my firsthand experience in surgery centers is that the directors of nursing were really doing all the accreditation work.

I have also seen credentialing listed as a duty in medical director agreements. Once again though, my firsthand experience is that credentialing is primarily a clerical task. An administrative assistant can search for providers in the various online databases, collect documents from the providers' offices, and file all the paperwork in folders. My experience is that medical directors often take minutes to review a credentialing file.

One of the duties you can put in a medical directorship agreement is attendance at regular meetings. Some examples include:

- Quality Assurance meetings

- Process Improvement meetings

- Medical Executive Committee / Medical Peer Review meetings

- Board of Directors meetings

Medical directorships are usually compensated on an hourly basis with an hourly rate multiplied by the number of hours worked. The agreements always set a maximum number of hours that will be paid. Any work performed in excess of the maximum hourly limit is not reimbursed. In determining what maximum hourly limit to set, you should consider the size of the operation compared to other operations. For example, if a hospital has an endoscopy medical director and they don't know how many hours they will need him or her to work, they can reference the number of hours worked by medical directors of other hospitals performing a similar number of endoscopies.

PROFESSIONAL MANAGEMENT AND CO-MANAGEMENT

There is a long history of third-party management companies operating hospitals, physician practices, surgery centers, endoscopy centers, home health agencies, dialysis centers, imaging centers, and vascular access centers that they do not wholly own. As it relates to physician alignment, it is also common for physicians and physician practices to provide management services to hospital-owned outpatient businesses and/or joint ventures.

An important distinction to make is the difference between professional, business-oriented management arrangements and clinical co-management arrangements. Generally, professional management services are nonclinical business services that could be provided by non-physicians.

Clinical co-management services are provided entirely by physicians. Clinical co-management arrangements are performance-based arrangements whereby hospitals compensate physicians to manage the quality and efficiency of one or more service lines. Clinical co-managements surpass traditional medical directorships in two respects.

1. While traditional directorships engage one physician for each service line, clinical co-management arrangements engage multiple physicians for each service line.

2. While traditional directorships compensate physicians on an hourly basis, regardless of outcomes, clinical co-management arrangements reward the achievement of predefined clinical outcomes with incentive compensation.

Clinical co-management is often used in inpatient and outpatient hospital service lines such as cardiology and orthopedics, as well as to engage physicians selling ambulatory surgery centers after the sale. When physicians sell a business to a hospital, such as a surgery center or imaging center, the physicians can immediately lose interest in working there. One common feature of management and co-management arrangements is the noncompete clause. It is fairly common for the contractor to be prohibited from planning or investing in a competing business during the course of the contract and for a two-year period after it expires.

Clinical co-management arrangements sometimes involve a joint venture management company that is co-owned by many physicians and may also include hospital ownership. Alternatively, the hospital may engage physicians directly as contractors without creating a joint venture management company. At least one-third of the total compensation is usually put at risk for the achievement of predefined clinical quality goals.

Differences in Types of Management Arrangements

	Non-Physician Professional Business Management	Pay-for-Performance Physician Clinical Management	Clinical Co-Management
Structure	Direct Management Contract	Direct Management Contract	Management company is a physician–hospital joint venture
Fees	Fee based on 3% - 6% of service revenue	Fee based on services provided with >30% of fee at risk for performance metrics	

Generally speaking, the term "management" can create a fair amount of confusion when referring to these types of arrangements. Clinical co-management arrangements may involve higher hourly physician compensation rates than typical medical directorships, but there is also a pay-for-performance component.

Example Professional Management Arrangement Duties

1. Prepare agenda and material for quarterly management meeting.

2. Prepare center's financial statements monthly.

3. Prepare operational reports with volumes and trending monthly.

4. Provide access to benchmarking tools and peer support.

5. Provide administrator (management company employee passed through to client at cost).

6. Provide access to corporate staff in revenue cycle management, material management, business development, and human resources.

Example Physician Management and Co-Management Pay-for-Performance Metrics

1. First case on-time start percentage.

2. Achieve average room turnover times <30 minutes.

3. Maintain 0% infection rate.

4. Maintain >95% patient satisfaction rate on surveys.

Other important distinctions to make include the following:

1. Professional management companies tend to employ the center administrator and pass through their salaries and benefits at cost to their clients.

2. Billing services are usually separate and distinct from management services. As an example, a management company might charge 6% of the center's revenue for professional management services and an additional 4% of revenue for billing services. The total fees are 10% of revenue.

3. There should be no redundancy in the duties of the management company and the duties of the administrator, medical director, and director of nursing. If the director of nursing's job description indicates that the person is responsible for the center's ongoing accreditation with TJC, then that is an employee's duty, not the management company's duty. Similarly, if quality assurance or process improvement duties are included in the medical director agreement, then those are medical director duties, not

management company duties.

4. Dictation, coding, information system support, facility maintenance, equipment preventive maintenance, and many other services tend to be provided by third-party vendors, not the management company.

There is a fair amount of public information on professional management arrangements. There are several dozen management companies that specialize in surgery centers, endoscopy centers, imaging centers, dialysis centers, and vascular access centers.

Professional Management Companies

ASCs	Endo Centers	Imaging Centers	Dialysis Centers	Vascular Access
SCA	Physician's Endoscopy	RadNet	DaVita	Fresenius Vascular Care
USPI	AmSurg	MedQuest Associates	Fresenius	Lifeline Vascular Access
AmSurg		Alliance Healthcare		Vascular Access Centers

Pure "business" management companies may or may not require an equity ownership in the centers they manage. Some of the publicly traded companies will require a majority ownership interest so they can consolidate financials.

CLINICAL SERVICES PSAS

Professional Service Arrangements (PSAs) is a catchall term used to identify a variety of arrangements that do not fall into one of the other major types of arrangements described herein. Some of the types of PSAs include:

1. Reimbursement paid to physicians for performance of specific services with predefined rates by CPT code. For example:

a. Hearing screening tests performed by neonatologists on infants. Neonatologists sometimes have difficulty collecting fees for these services from Medicaid. Hospitals and neonatologists enter into an agreement whereby the neonatologists only accept payment from the hospital and do not bill insurance or patients for the services.

b. Emergency department visits and occupational health services performed by physicians on hospital employees. The hospital wants to pay 100% of the costs related to work-related injuries so their injured employees have no out-of-pocket expenses. Therefore, they circumvent insurance and contract directly for a predetermined fee.

2. Reimbursement paid to physicians for a limited number of related services based on a predefined work RVU rate.

a. Gastroenterologists agree to be compensated on a work RVU rate for their professional fees for services rendered in a hospital-owned surgery center. The payor mix is heavily weighted with self-pay and Medicaid, and the physicians could otherwise not afford to treat that population of patients. The hospital compensates the physicians and bills insurance on the physicians' behalf.

c. Interventional radiology services performed by radiologists on hospital patients. The radiology group that provides coverage at the hospital has radiologists who can also provide interventional radiology services. The hospital wants to guarantee payment for interventional radiology services on a work RVU basis. The physician only accepts payment from the hospital and does not bill insurance or patients for the services. The hospital bills insurance on the physicians' behalf.

3. Compensation paid to physicians for clinical services or coverage on the basis of a predefined hourly rate.

   a. A rural hospital operates a family clinic and compensates multiple primary care physicians in the region to cover the various shifts. The physicians accept compensation for hours worked based on an hourly rate. The hospital bills insurance for the services.

4. Reimbursement paid to physicians for a wide range of services based on a predefined work RVU rate.

   a. A group of rural physicians treat a patient population that is approximately 50% Medicare, Medicaid, and self-pay patients. The physicians' work volume exceeds the 90th percentile, but their collections per work RVU approximate the 25th percentile. Rather than become hospital employees, the group and a hospital enter into an agreement wherein the group assigns all collections to the hospital and the hospital compensates the group on a fixed work RVU rate for clinical services performed.

Generally speaking, PSAs need to have the same three basic elements of any contractual service arrangement between physicians and hospitals.

Most PSAs are driven by the need for physician services in spite of suboptimal reimbursement that would otherwise preclude them. Large-scale PSAs are being used more and more often as quasi-employment arrangements. As discussed later, physician employment arrangements can have several downsides. PSAs are more advantageous to physicians than employment arrangements in several respects. The three main advantages for physicians are summarized in the following list.

1. PSAs tend to be easier to unwind. The practice's legal entity is intact, so both the physicians and hospital can return to the way things were before if it doesn't work out. Either party can cancel the agreement.

2. Independent physicians who sell their practices to hospitals normally sign noncompete agreements that prevent them from practicing medicine in the area for several years after their hospital employment agreement is terminated. Noncompetes protect the hospitals' investment in the practice purchases. Physicians have to either renew their employment agreements or move out of the community when the agreements expire.

3. If physicians sell their practices to a hospital before entering an employment agreement, then they may have to buy their practices back from the hospital if they want to go back into private practice in the same community. This may not even be an option if the hospital enforces their noncompetes.

As noted above, PSAs are easier to unwind. The main benefits of PSAs are operational alignments and mitigation of future reimbursement risk.

GAINSHARING

Gainsharing, now sometimes referred to as shared savings, refers to an arrangement between physicians and a hospital, whereby a hospital agrees to share money associated with reductions in the cost of care created by the efforts of the physicians. For example, it may be prearranged that an orthopedic group would be compensated for 40% of any cost reductions it generates by substituting expensive implants used during knee and hip surgeries with more cost effective implants (of equal quality) from alternative vendors.

In 1999, the OIG issued a Special Advisory Bulletin taking the position that gainsharing arrangements violated the civil monetary penalty (CMP) provision banning hospitals from paying physicians to limit patient care.[47] However, since 1999 the OIG has individually reviewed and approved thirteen gainsharing arrangements and one pay-for-performance program through published advisory opinions. These advisory opinions describe the OIG's rationale for approving each arrangement and have created a considerable framework for each new arrangement submitted for the OIG's review.

Additionally, the Medicare Shared Savings Program (MSSP) for Accountable Care Organizations (ACOs) grants gainsharing waivers to ACO participants under the Shared Savings Distribution waiver. This means that ACOs can distribute shared savings generated by the efforts of participating providers under certain parameters without violating the CMP.

NONCLINICAL ARRANGEMENTS

There are numerous other arrangements that various organizations use to align themselves with physicians. Many of the professional service arrangements discussed in this chapter involve a hospital paying a physician for a service that only a physician could provide.

The following arrangements do not fit so neatly into such a definition. These services may be provided by physicians to hospitals or by hospitals to physicians, or third parties may be involved. These services also do not necessarily require the skills or abilities of licensed physicians. Many of these services may be commonly provided by ordinary business people.

Staff Leasing (Professional Employer Organization) Services

Staff leasing is deployed in healthcare settings in several ways.

Physicians Staff Leasing to Hospitals

Physicians employ teams of specialized staff that they lease to hospitals. For example, a physician group leases dozens of surgical assistants to hospitals. While surgical assistants are commonly used, reimbursement for surgical assistant services is only about 15% of the physician reimbursement rates for the same procedures.

The hospitals in question save appreciable money on surgical assistants because employees of the physician group do not have to have the same costly benefits as hospital employees and the cost is spread over multiple hospitals. This makes the provision of surgical assistants less costly, and the surgeons who use them at the hospitals love it because it makes surgeries quicker and easier.

Physicians Leasing Staff to Surgery Centers

Physician practices lease their business office staff to endoscopy centers and surgery centers on the days their physicians are operating. This is a common strategy for Amsurg—one of the largest surgery center operators in the United States, which leases about 29% of its center staff from physician practices. For small single-specialty centers, this split-staffing model saves both the practices and surgery centers from having idle staff when the physician is not present.

Hospitals Leasing Staff to Physicians

Hospitals may lease staff to physician groups. For example, a neonatology group may lease neonatal nurse practitioners from the hospital to which they provided services.

In these staff leasing arrangements, employee salaries, benefit costs, and payroll costs are usually passed through from one party to the other on a cost basis plus a small margin for the administrative costs of being the employer of record.

Electronic Medical Records Subsidies

There is a Stark Law exception, matched in the Anti-Kickback Statute, that allows hospitals and health systems to provide electronic medical record (EMR) systems to independent physician practices at less than the cost the hospital paid to acquire the EMR system. Providing products or services to physicians below market prices normally can be construed as a kickback. However, legislators have allowed this to occur to encourage the use of EMRs and the interconnectivity of hospital and physician medical records that might otherwise be cost-prohibitive for many physician practices. The original exceptions and safe harbors were recently extended through the year 2021.

The Stark Law and Anti-Kickback Statute allow hospitals to write off or subsidize 85% of the allocated cost of EMR systems provided to physicians. In other words, independent physician practices can pay as little as 15% of the actual cost of the EMR system they use when it is provided to them by a local hospital or health system.

This is a big deal for several reasons:

1.   It saves patients and insurance companies money. The ability to instantly access patient history and physical records, lab results, imaging, and inpatient and outpatient records is huge from an efficiency standpoint. Having all of a patient's information available saves repeated visits and costs associated with duplicate testing.

2.   Many physician practices could not afford to pay full price for a medical record system. Reduced-cost EMR systems save practices money while keeping them up-to-date technologically.

3.   The interconnectivity propaganda is actually true in this case. Once a physician practice switches over to a highly subsidized EMR system, there is little chance it will switch to another EMR at a significantly higher cost. This ties the physicians to the hospital, and hospitals always want to have as many relationships with community physicians as they can.

Colorado Children's Hospital in Denver, Colorado, markets its PedsConnect system to independent pediatric physician practices in the greater Denver area. The practices can access the system through the Internet using Citrix, a remote access tool. The practices pay an affordable annual fee to use the system, and they don't have to lay out $100,000 or more to purchase and install their own hardware and software systems in their offices. This savings is augmented by a Stark Law exception that permits hospitals to write off, or absorb, up to 85% of the costs of such systems. Under this federal fraud exception, hospitals can effectively give electronic hardware and software system access to physician practices at 85% off the retail price. If the physicians were to buy these systems themselves, they would have to pay full price.

Again, it seems like a no-brainer, right? I can get a very expensive software and hardware system for my practice at 85% off the regular price if I enter into a usage contract with Regional Health System to piggyback on their system. Why would any physician practices pay full price when they can pay 15 cents on the dollar to their local hospital?

This Applications Service Provider (ASP) model is not just affordable; it is also very strategically smart in that it makes independent practices reliant on a particular hospital or health system and accustoms them to using particular systems. It is expensive to install your own EMR system, and it is hugely inconvenient from the perspective that it takes physicians and staff about a year to get up to speed in using a new system. Additionally, if you use a different system than the local hospital, you have to pay to get computer software interfaces so the two systems can talk to each other. Interface costs are just salt in the wound. In aggregate, practices that start using their hospital's system are not likely to go out and drop hundreds of thousands of dollars to buy their own system. The switching costs are too high from a financial and logistical perspective.

Managed Service Organizations and PHOs

Managed service organizations (MSOs) provide business services to physician practices, while the physicians remain independent.

For example, a managed service organization may provide:

- Management services at 5% of revenues

- Billing and collection at 4% of revenues

- Office staff at cost plus a 3% administrative fee

- Office space

- Payor contracting services

- Access to and maintenance of a practice management system for scheduling and an electronic medical record system for patient records

I like to think of MSOs as a contractual outsourcing service for physicians. Physicians can outsource all of the responsibilities of managing the business side of their practices to a third party. The physician focuses on practicing medicine and the MSO takes a percentage of the fees the physician generates as compensation. If the MSO does a bad job, the physician can fire them and walk away.

MSOs are a good model in states where the CPM laws are strict and a quasi-physician employment model is needed.

California has the strictest interpretation of the CPM doctrine of all states. The only exception that allows physicians to work for non-physicians is through the employment of a not-for-profit foundation. Therefore, MSOs are very common in California.

PHOs (physician–hospital organizations) are similar to MSOs but just provide payor contracting services. Health insurance companies will sometimes contract with a collective group of medical providers through a unified PHO. Doing this reduces the administrative burden of having to do 100 different negotiations, and strengthens the negotiating power of the providers because they are contracting as a collective group.

Revenue Cycle: Billing and Collections

Billing and collections services may be provided by a hospital to a physician-owned business or vice versa. Hospitals may provide billing services to physician-owned surgery centers and/or imaging centers when needed as well. The revenue cycle includes several key duties.

Buyers will want the billing entity to provide as much of the revenue cycle duties as possible. These include:

- Dictation/Transcription
- Coding
- Charge Entry
- Clearinghouse
- Payment Posting
- Account Follow-Up Calls
- Patient Statements and Postage
- Billing System Software

There has been a marked increase in hospital-affiliated MSOs and even large physician groups providing centralized management, revenue cycle services, information systems, and EMR services to independent physician practices. Epic, All Scripts, GE Centricity, and a plethora of other practice management and EMR systems can be very expensive, with a substantial upfront cost followed by annual licensing and maintenance costs for the life of the system.

Free information systems for billing clients

Zotec Partners in Indianapolis, Indiana, provides outsourced billing services to 6,000 physicians in all 50 U.S. states. The company specializes in radiology, anesthesiology, and pathology practices.

Part of the reason Zotec has been so successful is that it provides its billing clients with a hosted information and billing system. This is a huge cost savings for physician practices, and hardly any billing companies provide this type of benefit. Providing IT services for physician practices saves the practices real money on purchasing servers, software licenses, help desk support, and system upgrades, which tend to be needed every three years or so. Why does Zotec throw in the kitchen sink and give its billing clients information systems?

Zotec's business model hinges on the fact that it can provide billing services much more cost-effectively and efficiently when all of its clients, or most of them at least, use the same billing systems and practice management systems. If all of Zotec's billing staff only has to use one billing and information system for all practices, it saves tremendously on staff training because any biller in the company can perform work for any practice client the company has.

Zotec's turnkey billing and information systems model makes a lot of sense, and I expect to see more of it in the coming years.

Equipment and Building Leases

Hospitals and physicians will frequently lease equipment and real estate to each other. This may include such equipment as C-arms, surgical instruments, lithotripters, ultrasound machines, and similar mobile devices, as well as building leases for office space, imaging centers, or surgery centers.

I have found that some physicians are very keen on owning real estate. I have also met many physicians who own vacant office buildings that they can't lease.

As with all types of deals in this book, it is important that the pricing for leases be set at market rates. The parties can't enter into terms that are more or less favorable than what could be procured from an independent financial company.

Similarly, it is not commercially reasonable for a surgery center to lease a lithotripter from a urologist-owned company 1,000 times per year and pay $1,000 for each use. While the $1,000 usage rate may indeed be a reasonable market price for using a lithotripter, the total cost of this arrangement is $1.0 million per year, while the surgery center could purchase its own lithotripter for $500,000. This is an example of how an arrangement could be reasonably priced but still fail a commercial reasonableness test.

Midlevels, Physician-Extenders

Midlevel professional providers (midlevels) include nurse practitioners, physician assistants, audiologists, and physical, speech, and occupational therapists. Midlevels are licensed healthcare professionals who may work independently or under the supervision of physicians. Midlevels are sometimes referred to as physician extenders because they can be staffed to cost-effectively support a physician's practice of medicine.

For instance, internal medicine, family practice, and OBGYN

physician practices commonly employ nurse practitioners (NPs), while neurologists and orthopedic surgeons may employ physician assistants (PAs). NPs and PAs can perform patient evaluations and office visits themselves. This is a big deal because most insurance companies will pay 85% of the normal physician office visit rate when an NP or PA performs the office visit and bills under their own name. The economics of this payment arrangement are great for physician practices because they can get 85% of a normal physician payment using an NP or PA who only costs the practice 30% to 40% of what a physician would cost.

If the practice bills on an "incident to" basis, then they will collect 100% of the physician payment rate for visits performed by midlevels. "Incident to" standards require the physicians to be more involved in the evaluation because the services are being billed under the physician's name and not the midlevel's.

There are practices where internal medicine physicians make $700,000 to $1.0 million or more per year because they employ multiple midlevel providers for each physician. The practices make lots of money on the midlevels because they pay them much less than they collect for the services they render to their patients. Some practices net $200,000 or more per midlevel after paying them all their salaries and benefits.

Similarly, it is common for ENT physicians to employ audiologists and speech therapists, and it is common for orthopedic surgeons to employ physical therapists. These types of clinicians can only accept patient referrals from the physicians of their employer. This is known as the in-office ancillary exception. Physicians can refer patients to designated health services they own if the sole source of patient referrals is that practice. Such office-based clinics cannot accept patient referrals from other physician practices.

Development Services

Development services include business start-up activities that may be performed by physicians or for physicians by another party. Such development services include medical facility planning and design, construction management, state survey preparation, accreditation survey preparation, Medicare survey preparation, equipment planning and procurement, and various other duties.

Physicians may be performing development services for a hospital-owned surgery center or imaging center, or for an inpatient facility. Alternatively, a hospital may perform development services for a joint venture or wholly physician-owned business.

Development services sometimes do not require the specific skill set of a physician, but physicians may certainly have valuable input since they are usually the end user of the healthcare facilities they are developing.

The one-to-two-year process of designing, building, and opening an ambulatory surgery center or imaging center may cost hundreds of thousands of dollars when rendered by a professional ASC or imaging management company. This range only applies to the time and expertise of the "owner's rep" or project manager who is overseeing the development process. The hands-on work is being done by architects, engineers, interior designers, developers, the general construction manager, subcontractors, and vendors. It may cost $5 million, or much more, to develop the entire medical facility. Development services are just the management aspects of this process.

The time and cost can vary significantly based on whether a new facility is being built, whether an existing facility needs improvements to bring it up to code, what the state licensing requirements are, and how backed up the accrediting agency is at the time. If physicians are providing these services, and it is the first time they have been involved in such a process, it could very well take longer and cost more. Professional development companies perform this process over and over again.

Alternatively, having physicians perform development keeps them engaged in a process that would be drawn out for years anyway. A common complaint among physicians is that they did not have adequate, or any, input into the development of hospital facilities. A hospital administrator does not want to develop a facility that will be used 15 years or more and have the physician users be unhappy with it. Physician engagement is a key element of joint ventures. It may be worth the extra time and money to have physicians perform development services when the occasion arises.

Imaging Pre-Authorization

When a physician orders a major imaging test like an MRI or a CT scan, commercial insurers may require the procedures to be pre-authorized. This means the physician's office has to call the insurance company or go online and request permission to order the test. If the pre-authorization is not performed, then the insurance company has the right to not pay for the test.

While pre-authorizations for imaging are traditionally the responsibility of the physician's office, some imaging centers offer pre-authorization services to ordering physician practices as a value-added service. The ordering physicians' practices may be inclined to use an imaging center that performs pre-authorizations for them because it frees up the physician's office staff to work on other things.

Catered Meals

No American physician will ever starve to death. The amount of free food in the healthcare industry is unbelievable. Free meals are provided at hospital meetings, board meetings, and committee meetings. I had a practice manager who couldn't schedule a meeting with me and her physician unless I could bring lunch for the office staff—I didn't.

The Sunshine Act has imposed new rules requiring all drug and device manufacturers to report every payment and dollar spent on physicians. This law does not apply to hospitals, and it does not mean that manufacturers cannot provide meals to physicians. This law just imposes a transparency requirement so the public can identify what physicians are receiving compensation like catered meals.

Borrowed Equipment and Instruments

It is not uncommon for a physician-owned surgery center or physician practice to occasionally borrow an instrument set or a piece of minor equipment from a hospital. These arrangements are often informal, without written agreements or compensation arrangements.

Mileage Reimbursement

It is fairly common for employed physicians' mileage to be reimbursed for travel to secondary facilities or for travel for consultations or medical director services provided to secondary healthcare facilities.

For example, a specialist who regularly rounds on nursing home patients or homecare patients will likely be reimbursed for his or her mileage related to travel to and from the various facilities and patient homes they visited.

Chapter 5
Physician Employment Deals

OVERVIEW

This chapter discusses the following topics related to physician employment:

- Increases in Physician Practice Sales

- Accountable Care Organizations and Practice Acquisitions

- Why Do New Physicians Choose Employment?

- Why Do Established Physicians Choose Employment?

- Who Buys Physician Practices and Why?

- Physician Employment Structure

- Employment Agreement

- Full-Time Hospitalists

- Physician Practice Consolidation

- Career Changes

- Work RVU Obsession and Physician Payment Reform

INCREASES IN PHYSICIAN PRACTICE SALES

Around the time the stock market crashed in late 2008 and early 2009, hospitals started buying up physician practices en mass again. I say again because this happened before, in the 1990s.

Healthcare costs got pretty high in the 1990s too. Employers and health insurers beat costs back down by rolling out HMO health plans to their enrollees. "Closed network" HMO plans restricted patients to a limited pool of low-cost physicians and medical facilities in their communities. Physicians were paid on a "capitated" basis. This meant that physicians were getting paid lump sums for taking care of thousands of patients rather than getting paid for every single little procedure they performed for each patient. Patients lost personal choice, but they gained affordable healthcare.

Around this time, many hospitals started buying physician practices. I remember getting into a fairly contentious argument the first time I ever spoke to a hospital executive about his organization buying physician practices. I couldn't get a clear answer on how they justified paying millions of dollars for physician practices that had very few assets and generated no cash flow for anyone but the physicians.

A fundamental difference with physician practice acquisitions this time around is that the prices paid for physician practices are much lower than they were in the 1990s. Whereas physicians received millions of dollars for their practices in the 1990s, most of the sales occurring now are just buying assets and medical records.

I don't want to give the impression that hospitals did not employ physicians prior to 2008. Some health systems have been employing physicians for years. ProMedica Health in Toledo is one example of a hospital system that has been building up its multispecialty physician practice for over 10 years and now has over 300 physicians.

ACCOUNTABLE CARE ORGANIZATIONS AND PRACTICE ACQUISITIONS

A hybrid of the fee-for-service payment model and the capitated HMO model has been implemented on a major national scale in the form of *Accountable Care Organizations* (ACOs), and hospitals have bought thousands of physician practices to prepare. In the 1990s, primary care physicians served as gatekeepers and more or less controlled patients' access to specialists and ancillary services. Staying true to the old model, the majority of the physician practice acquisitions in recent years have been primary care practices.

The new Medicare ACO model, which already has 400 major healthcare organization participants, stipulates that providers and physicians will be paid on a fee-for-service basis, as they are now, but they will be entitled to a bonus of up to 50% to 60% of the cost savings they create. So providers like physicians and hospitals still get paid more for treating more patients, but they also get a bonus when their average per member per month cost is lower than a predefined benchmark.

This ACO model is unique in that it marries the HMO "per member per month" model with the traditional fee-for-service model, thereby encouraging providers to be productive and treat lots of patients, but it also rewards them for keeping the average cost down overall for the entire patient population. The determinant of success will likely be dependent on where the government sets the benchmark target for average patient costs. If the benchmark is set too low, it will be too difficult to earn the bonus.

There are over 600 Medicare and commercial ACOs at the time of this book's publishing.

WHY DO NEW PHYSICIANS CHOOSE EMPLOYMENT?

After four years of undergraduate college, four years of medical school, and three-to-five years of residency and fellowships, it is no wonder than new physicians don't want to live another two to three years with little or no compensation while they try to build up their new practices. An offer to work for someone else for a fair amount of money to start seems like a pretty good deal.

The costs to start a new practice are surprisingly high. Office lease space, computer systems, software, malpractice insurance, and office staff are not cheap. This is a tough hurdle for a medical student who has just incurred $200,000 in student loan debt.

While the salary potential is higher over the long term for practice owners, the initial years are rough. This is pushing more new physicians into employment arrangements.

WHY DO ESTABLISHED PHYSICIANS CHOOSE EMPLOYMENT?

I met a practice manager of a general surgery group that had been approached multiple times by potential hospital buyers. They never consummated any of these opportunities because they could not come to terms with the potential buyers. The practice manager told me, "You can only kill the golden goose once," implying that if you're going to sell, you can only do it once so you better get the best deal you can.

My observations are that there are two main types of physician practice sales to hospitals. The first type consists of physician practices that have no choice and must sell because they are not financially solvent. Periodically, I hear about a group of doctors who are earning $90,000 to $130,000 each per year. While this is a decent salary for most lay people, this is pretty poor for physicians. Even the average family practice physicians are earning $200,000. It is difficult for physicians to rationalize running their own independent practices when they can become employees and get paid more to do less work. For these types of practice sales, it is common for the purchase price to be very small. A $10,000 offer for minor equipment and furniture is not uncommon.

The second type consists of physicians of advancing years who are looking to sell the practice "business" they have built up over 30 years. They see this as cashing in and easing themselves into retirement. These physicians intend to spend their last three to five years in the practice slowly transitioning their patients over to younger physician recruits the hospital has hired. They can expect to receive a lump sum payment for the sale of their practice and perhaps a short employment contract.

WHO BUYS PHYSICIAN PRACTICES AND WHY?

The primary acquirers of existing physician practices are definitely hospitals and health systems.

There's been a big grab for physicians lately for a handful of reasons:

1. Physician reimbursement has been fairly flat. Except for a few specialties that have had specific increases or decreases, the net sustainable growth rate has been flat since 2003. With flat reimbursement and inflating costs, operating small practices is an uphill battle, and many physicians see employment as a solution.

2. Bigger practices that had the capital to purchase EMRs have done so. This makes it even harder for smaller practices that couldn't afford EMRs to compete for several reasons.

   a. Practices with EMRs operate with fewer office staff and lower costs. I was recently advised of an eight-physician practice that eliminated over 10 office staff positions after they implemented their EMR. They saved immense time and resources by eliminating all the paper charts and subsequent filing and lab paperwork.

b. Practices with EMRs that integrate with local hospitals are going to be preferential choices for hospitalist arrangements, on-call coverage, collection guarantees, and other professional service arrangements because the patients' medical information will flow back and forth between the hospitals and practices seamlessly.

c. There are general operational benefits from EMRs. Claims can be coded and submitted the same day services were performed. Physician and midlevel productivity can be easily measured. Clinical research can be more easily performed.

3. The reasons cited above have ultimately resulted in physicians, especially in small practices, working more for less compensation. There is a threshold for every business owner, including physicians, where it no longer makes sense for them to own their own business. More and more physicians are abandoning their practices for a steady paycheck and predictable workload.

The practical benefits of hospitals or health systems owning physician practices are threefold. First, while employed physicians are still able to make whatever medical decisions they see fit, there is a strong tendency for employed physicians to refer patients for imaging, labs, therapies, and surgical specialists that are affiliated with their employer. While some of this is undoubtedly attributed to loyalty, there are more utilitarian convenience factors as well. If the practice's EMR is connected to the imaging, lab, and other ancillary providers in the network, then it is more efficient for the practice to coordinate care when they are involved.

Second, hospitals can regulate hospitalist and on-call coverage better when coverage is a required part of their physician employment contracts. On-call coverage arrangements with independent physicians are subject to frequent renegotiations, pricing based on competitive heresy, competing availability of physicians, and the willingness of physicians to treat self-pay and Medicaid patients. Assigning employed physicians to provide this coverage is an ideal solution because they are perfectly willing to provide coverage when they are not at risk for their fees.

Third, buying physician practices is a competitive move. If a competing hospital buys the local general surgery group, all of a sudden those surgeons may stop performing surgeries at your hospital and terminate their emergency department on-call agreement with your facility. Now that you have no general surgery coverage, ambulances must divert incoming patients directly to your competitor hospital because they know that you don't have coverage.

PHYSICIAN EMPLOYMENT STRUCTURE

Physician employment contracts are organized somewhat differently than the joint venture operating agreements I described earlier. If the physician owned his or her own practice before becoming an employee, there will likely be a purchase agreement and an employment agreement

Major Components of Physician Practice Purchase Agreements

This section describes the major components of physician practice purchase plans.

Consideration (Price)

While you might think the price paid for physician practices is the primary negotiating term, this typically places second or third to the future physician compensation plans and noncompete clause.

For many physician practices there is no profitability to their "business" because the physicians keep most or all of the practice profit as their compensation. Because the physicians usually want to make the same amount of money (or more) going forward as employees, forward-looking projections reflect losses for the new owner unless the physicians volunteer to take pay cuts from what they have made historically.

Subsequently, physician practices may have little business value assigned to them other than their relatively few assets, including tables, desks, a few computers, and copy machines. Some specialist practices have diagnostic equipment that may add appreciable value, such as MRIs, ultrasound machines, DEXA scan machines, and other devices. A physician with a decent business consultant will argue that his or her practice also has intangible value and try to get compensated for things like workforce-in-place.

Identify Assets

As with any purchase agreement, the parties should clearly identify in writing exactly what is being purchased and the associated prices. A purchase agreement will typically have a list of all the assets that are included and excluded from the sale.

Equipment

A good place to start for equipment is the fixed asset register maintained by the practice's accountant. An on-site inspection of the equipment by an expert may be advisable if the item descriptions on the fixed asset register are too vague. The buyer and seller should both review the final list and identify exactly what is included and excluded from the sale.

Inventory will usually be exchanged based on a physical count of the supplies on hand when the sale is consummated.

Real Estate, Leasehold Improvements, and Lease Terms

It needs to be clearly identified whether the physician practice office space is a lease with a third party, a lease from a physician-owned real estate holding company, or if the building is owned by the practice itself.

If the practice is to remain in the same location, and the building is owned by the physicians, or a subset thereof, then the parties may need to negotiate a new building lease contract. This can be a very important deal point for buildings that are still being financed or require major maintenance.

Similarly, if the building is leased from an unrelated third party, it needs to be determined if the building improvements are owned by the practice or the landlord. Some practices have made hundreds of thousands of dollars of building improvements at their own expense. The parties need to determine if these improvements will be part of the purchase value and to what extent.

Noncompete Restrictions

Noncompete agreements are intended to provide the buyer with some protection from competitive threats that the seller may impose as a potential competitor. For example, if Dr. Jobs sold her practice to St. Mary's Medical Center for $300,000, and then started another practice across the street, she might capture 60% or more of the patients from her old group.

St. Mary's Medical Center could make far less money on its purchase than originally anticipated. For this reason, nearly all physician practice sales are performed with a two-to-three year employment agreement and noncompete restrictions preventing the physician from competing with the hospital acquirer for at least several years after the agreement has been terminated.

The mile radius of the noncompete is closely related to the

characteristics of the market, but a typical noncompete agreement may require a five mile noncompete radius for up to two years after the termination of the employment agreement.

Debt and Other Liabilities

It is important to identify at the onset what liabilities, if any, will be transferred during a sale. The buyer may structure its offer to include or exclude some or all of the debt. This should be spelled out in the purchase agreement.

If the buyer is not assuming the debt, it is expected that the seller will pay off the debts out of the proceeds paid. Some common liabilities that may be included or excluded are lines of credit, construction and tenant improvement loans, and equipment leases or related debt.

Debt is of particular importance if the physicians are selling for financial reasons. For example, Dr. Nguyen may be selling his practice, in part, because his declining service revenues are making it difficult for him to make payments on the construction loan he used to finance office space renovations. If the purchase offer for his practice is less than the amount he owes on the construction loan, then he will have to pay the balance of the loan off himself from his future salary.

Employment Agreement

Job Description

The job description should identify the physician's responsibilities and accountabilities in understandable terms. In general terms, the employer's expectations for hours worked and the nature of the services provided should be defined.

Performance Evaluation Criteria

Qualitative and objective performance criteria should be defined with the associated performance metrics. If there is a qualitative component to the performance evaluation, it should be defined in discrete terms and the person who will perform the assessment should be identified.

Compensation Model

Many different physician compensation models can built with a few basic elements. Variations of fixed-base salaries, work RVU production incentives, quality incentives, compensation maximums, call pay, medical directorships, and other professional service arrangements may be used.

On-Call Requirements

A major benefit of employing physicians is that hospitals can include unpaid call requirements in their employment agreements. The number of unpaid and paid call days should be clearly spelled out in the agreement. For example, an employment contract may require five days of unpaid call per month with compensation of $400 per day for each additional day of call beyond five days.

Paid Time Off

The number of vacation days, sick days, and leave of absence terms should be identified in the employment agreement. It should also be clear how much paid time off physicians can accrue if they don't use their time. For example, if Dr. Leatherman only takes three of her six weeks of time off each year, will she be able to keep the three weeks she does not use?

Noncompete

The noncompete discussed in the purchase agreement section may show up again in the employment agreement.

There have been several instances during the last few years when the Federal Trade Commission has gotten involved in the enforceability of physician noncompete restrictions. This comes into play when a single hospital employs the vast majority of physicians in a certain specialty. For example, if General Hospital employs all the cardiologists in Mayberry, then General Hospital not only has a monopoly on cardiology, but they can use the noncompete restriction in the cardiologists' employment agreements to prevent anyone from even trying to compete with them.

Dispute Resolution

Like most legal contracts, employment agreements usually have a clause that requires the parties to use a third-party arbitrator for dispute resolution prior to filing a legal complaint against the other party.

Compensation Stacks

Compensation stacks occur when a physician employee is being compensated for several components of services concurrently. An example would be an internal medicine physician working in a clinic setting who receives:

4. a fixed base salary

5. incentive compensation for wRVU production

6. on-call compensation of $300 per day

7. medical director compensation for oversight of a nursing

home

8. a quality bonus for achievement of patient satisfaction and operational goals

As you can imagine, a compensation arrangement that includes five different parts like this one raises the question of whether the individual components, which are each reasonable, collectively create an arrangement that is unreasonable.

FULL-TIME HOSPITALISTS

One relatively new employed physician role is the full-time hospitalist. Hospitalists are normally family practice or internal medicine physicians who have decided to dedicate themselves to exclusively treating patients who are admitted to a hospital. While most family medicine and internal medicine physicians have traditionally treated patients in their office and in a hospital setting, these new hospitalists focus strictly on hospital-based patients and do not maintain an office-based practice.

This developed in several ways:

1. A physician group realizes that it can stay busier by rounding on the hospital patients of other physicians. The physicians work out agreements with other physician groups and the hospital so they take care of all the hospitalized patients for several practices.

2. A family practice or internal medicine physician realizes his or her practice is becoming increasingly hospital-based and decides to focus just on that.

3. A hospital hires a physician with the sole intent for him or her to be an in-house physician.

PHYSICIAN PRACTICE CONSOLIDATION

Fear of impending Medicare physician payment reform has driven a lot of physicians out of private practice and into employment arrangements. Hospitals obviously have hired a lot of physicians while Kaiser and other large physician groups have also gotten bigger.

Congress has voted to delay Medicare physician payment cuts over ten years in a row. The cost of the annual "doc fix" is billions of dollars every year. Most authorities agree that physician payment reform is inevitable.

Larger groups achieve economies of scale and cost efficiencies that will allow them to continue to service Medicare patients in the future. Consolidating the costs of operating several separate physician offices into larger centralized clinics spreads their administrative costs better and enables more specialized administrative labor functions to develop within larger clinics.

Though physicians are prohibited from directly owning hospitals, they can still operate ambulatory surgery centers, cardiac catheterization labs, end-stage renal dialysis facilities, and radiation oncology facilities in competition with hospitals and health systems.

A major threat to hospitals is that these larger physician practice groups can accumulate the capital and management expertise to develop, acquire, and manage these ancillary healthcare services where they could not do so before. Lenders will be more inclined to finance new business ventures with large group practices of 50 to 100 physicians than they would be with small "one off" physician practices in the past.

Physician practice mergers are fairly sophisticated deals, and I've only seen a few occur. Combining different compensation models and determining each partner's new ownership in the combined practice is a complicated exercise.

The MSOs discussed in Chapter 4, "Contract Deals," have also become increasingly popular. I've recently observed an increase in hospital-owned MSOs and physician owned-MSOs. The large physician groups are well positioned to provide MSO services to small independent physician practices that want to remain independent. The MSO model may be a key strategic advantage when this generation of hospital-employed physicians decides that they want to go back into private practice.

CAREER CHANGES

I've met a number of individuals who strongly regretted becoming physicians. They spent seven to eight good years of their twenties and thirties getting trained and then realized that they really don't like what they do. Unfortunately for them, the debt accumulated during their training is difficult to pay off by anyone other than a physician, so they have to do it for some time.

I and several of my colleagues have met a number of physicians who were abandoning their medical practices to operate medical spas where they would administer fairly basic treatments like Botox injections. I distinctly recall a young general surgeon in California I met who chose to do exactly that after she finished her training.

Many physicians also make the jump to administration at hospitals, insurance companies, or consulting companies. Hospitals employ physicians as Chief Medical Officer, Director of Quality Improvement, and Director of Utilization Management. Virtually every health insurer in every state has a medical director who reviews denied medical claims for medical necessity. The healthcare consulting practices for the big-four accounting firms (Deloitte, Ernst & Young, PricewaterhouseCoopers, KPMG) as well as a number of fairly reputable consulting companies

(Accenture, Bain, Booz & Co, McKinsey) also employ physicians. In fact, it has been my experience that physicians working at consulting companies are almost always recruited at much higher positions and are promoted into senior positions faster than other employees who have been there for years.

WORK RVU OBSESSION AND PHYSICIAN PAYMENT REFORM

As discussed earlier, the United States is poised to venture away from fee-for-service payment arrangements and back into HMOs and capitated payment structures, as it did in the 1990s. The new catchphrase we're hearing everywhere is that healthcare is "shifting focus from volume to value."

Hospitals and home health agencies already moved to bundled, prospective payment systems in the 1980s and early 2000s for bundled inpatient stays (DRGs), outpatient services (APCs), and 60-day post-acute home healthcare (HHRGs).

Physicians, outpatient imaging centers, and ambulatory surgery centers have largely remained on fee-for-service payment structures. The HMO model in the 1990s paid physicians (mostly primary care) a fixed amount ("capitated basis") to serve a population of several thousand patients. They might receive, for example, $30 per member per month for a population of 1,000 patients. Of course, only a fraction of the patients would actually seek medical care, so it was up to the physicians to manage the population as they saw fit.

The catch was that capitation payment arrangements financially incentivized physicians to provide less care to their patients because the less cost the patients incurred, the more money the physicians got to keep. This is the closed network Kaiser model.

This is a curious structure because the Civil Monetary Penalty

Law imposes fines on a hospital or a critical access hospital that knowingly makes a payment, directly or indirectly, to a physician as an inducement to reduce or limit services provided with respect to individuals who are Medicare or Medicaid beneficiaries.

The work RVU productivity model is the most common among hospital-employed physicians. Physicians are guaranteed a base salary of, for example, $200,000 per year, for performing a minimum number of work RVUs—perhaps 3,800 work RVUs per year for an internal medicine physician. However, as the physician performs more than 3,800 work RVUs per year, the production rate of, for example, $50 per work RVU kicks in. So a physician performing 5,000 work RVUs per year at a $50 rate would earn about $250,000 per year. In addition to this, that physician might also be paid $15,000 for a nursing home medical directorship and $200 per day for on-call days taken in excess of the minimum 5 days per month.

While the work RVU model is extremely simple and easy to understand, it does not account for qualitative elements of a physician's practice. After all, two physicians in the same specialty who perform the same number of work RVUs per year could be very different in terms of the health of their patients and the operation of their practice. Surely the troubled physician who publicly demeans and criticizes the staff in front of patients because he is going through a painful divorce is not performing as well as his colleague who, while performing the same number of work RVUs, is also serving as a medical director of the indigent care clinic, training residents, conducting research, and presenting papers at conferences.

If you ask the administrator of a hospital physician network how they measure employed physicians' quality, the only response you will probably get is that they track the number of complaints filed against the physician and the results of patient satisfaction surveys. Patient satisfaction scores collected from voluntary surveys, by themselves, do not provide a complete assessment of a physician's performance. The following is a list of 69 qualitative factors that may contribute to a physician's perceived value to an employer, other than just work RVU production.

1. Experience leading and supervising staff

2. Experience leading and supervising other physicians

3. Medical director experience for a variety of disciplines and sub-disciplines

4. Research experience

5. Publications

6. Board certification(s)

7. Personality

8. Patient satisfaction scores

9. Staff satisfaction scores

10. On-call availability

11. Willingness to take more than 5 days of on call per month

12. Ability to serve in medical director roles

13. Clean liability claim history

14. Years practicing in the community

15. Fellowship training

16. Domestic training vs. foreign medical graduate

17. Languages spoken

18. Years since medical school

19. Years of post-residency experience

20. High severity coding tendencies

21. Past licensure suspensions

22. Pending litigation

23. Experience with electronic medical records

24. Experience with specific medical records systems

25. Physician honor society

26. Patient readmission rates

27. The occurrence of never events

28. Felony convictions

29. On-time appointment starts

30. On-time surgery starts

31. On-time dictation completion

32. Willingness to accept at-risk compensation

33. The percent of compensation willing to put at risk

34. Quality measures incorporated in contract

35. The number of quality measures in their contract

36. Contract length

37. Noncompete in their contract

38. Mile radius of the noncompete

39. Length of the noncompete

40. Employment contract renewal history

41. Teaching experience

42. Experience supervising residents

43. Program development experience

44. Governance experience (e.g., board of directors, medical executive committee, CQI committee, etc.,)

45. Litigation expert testimony experience

46. Speaking experience

47. Journal review or editor experience

48. Number of patient and staff complaints

49. Ivy league training

50. Internal training or affiliate training

51. Current employee renewal vs. replacement employee vs. market expansion hire

52. Health Professional Shortage Area;

53. Ability to travel

54. Schedule flexibility

55. Willingness to provide night and weekend coverage

56. Willingness to perform home visits

57. Need to relocate

58. Commuting distance

59. Performance of any/all indicator relative to peers

60. Multiple physicians hired as a group

61. Competitiveness in the market

62. Percent of employed physicians in the market

63. Percent of specialists employed in the market

64. The number of competing groups in the market

65. Responsibility for clinic and/or budgetary responsibility

66. Clinical trial experience

67. Peer review organization experience

68. Visits performed per day

69. Vaccination rates

This is just a sample list. There are dozens, if not hundreds, of more specific quality measures for specialists and surgeons. It is unfortunate that many of these qualitative measures go unused and that many physicians are being compensated solely on their work RVU production.

Future research is needed to delineate quantitative physician compensation from qualitative compensation and to ascribe value to the performance of these various attributes.

Oscar Wilde cleverly answered the question, "What is a cynic?" by replying that he is "[a] man who knows the price of everything and the value of nothing."

As a former appraiser, I have to admit that I made a living

knowing the price of everything. However, I have never seen, nor heard of risk-adjusted hospitalization rates, treatment adherence percentage, days on medication percentage, or patient mortalities being factored into any physician compensation arrangement.

Donald Berwick, CEO of the Institute for Healthcare Improvement, is fond of saying, "Every system is perfectly designed to achieve exactly the results it gets."

Naturally, this implies that if there is a problem in the results you are getting, you have to make a systematic change to get a different result. It won't fix itself.

PART II:
BIG PICTURE

Chapter 6
The Trouble with Monopolies

OVERVIEW

This chapter discusses the following topics related to healthcare competition in the United States:

- Mega Health Systems and Insurers: The New Ma Bells

- Insurance Consolidation

- Health System Consolidation

- Analogy: The Cathedral and the Bazaar

- Example: General Hospital Embraces the Bazaar

- Example: Regional Health System: The Cathedral Employs Physicians

MEGA HEALTH SYSTEMS AND INSURERS: THE NEW MA BELLS

One can't help but notice the similarities between the vertical and horizontal integration of health systems and health insurers in the United States and the organization of the original phone company, AT&T ("Mother Bell" or "Ma Bell"). The U.S. government blessed Ma Bell's monopoly on telecommunications in America largely because it was believed at the time that a single integrated telephone network was necessary to maintain a cost-effective and reliable telephone system.

Ma Bell argued, among other things, that the need to develop and maintain high quality, reliable systems and equipment that would last 20 or 30 years could not be achieved affordably by multiple competing phone companies. They said such long-term investments required a massive scale. The development of multiple phone networks would create huge cost redundancies and ultimately higher costs for consumers.

Much of the rationalization behind health system and insurance consolidation is the same. Hospitals and health systems merge to eliminate redundant overhead and administrative costs while achieving the scale necessary to allow for higher levels of labor specialization and efficiency. Incidentally, large health systems have more leverage in negotiations with health insurers because they represent more providers and a larger chunk of the market. The less competition there is, the more power they have to negotiate higher prices with health insurers.

Similarly, consolidating health insurers represent more employers, and subsequently, more patients. Health insurers also gain more negotiating power at the table when they represent 15%, 20%, or 30% of the patient population.

A Chicago-based health insurance executive once enthusiastically told me there were 80 hospitals in the greater Chicago area. He said, "There's lots of competition, and I love competition." This executive had many options as to what hospitals and physicians his company would let participate in their health insurance network. If a particular provider wanted more money than his competitors, the health insurer could tell him to take what they were offering or leave the network. There were many other alternatives for the health insurance company.

The Department of Justice tried repeatedly over the years to break up the Ma Bell monopoly. For years, however, the government and Ma Bell maintained a truce that provided that Ma Bell could maintain its monopoly over telecommunications as long as it did not compete in related fields such as electronics, computers, or other business and consumer products.

Ma Bell maintained total control over a long list of local phone companies while also having a monopoly on long-distance service. This arrangement is very similar to the Mega Health Systems' control over smaller regional health systems and individual hospitals, physicians, and ancillary services. It is also very similar to national health insurers' control over affiliate health plans in each state.

The downfall of Ma Bell and the rise of competitors like MCI and Motorola was largely the result of technological advances in radio communications and the development of the cellular network model. The cellular network model enabled MCI to develop its own telephone network at lower cost than Ma Bell without making the major capital investments that would have formerly been required to develop a phone network.

The MCI lawsuit gave the Justice Department the ammunition it needed to break up the Ma Bell monopoly and require it to spin off all of its local phone companies.

What they found after the monopoly was broken up was that Ma Bell didn't have the marketing expertise to sell its products and services in an open market. It had never needed to sell anything before and got its clock cleaned when it went head-to-head with the marketing and sales departments of its new competitors.

In this analogy, Kaiser is akin to MCI. Kaiser is an HMO-model health system based in California that has been very successful in developing and delivering a low-cost health plan. Kaiser, like other HMOs, is unique because not only does it own hospitals and employ physicians directly but it also sells its own health insurance.

Employers buy Kaiser health insurance for their employees, and their employees can primarily only see Kaiser physicians and go to Kaiser facilities for their care. This is the "closed network" HMO model. It is very effective in curbing costs. In an NPR article published in 2012, Kaiser's CEO, George Halvorson, said, "We're at least 10% better everywhere. Sometimes we're 15% to 20% less expensive."[48]

In California in 2011, Kaiser had a 31% market share of full service health plans from an enrollee standpoint and a 47% market share from a revenue standpoint.[49] Kaiser's revenue market share in California was equivalent to the market share of the next 16 largest health plans combined.

In Colorado, the Kaiser Foundation Health Plan's market share is 25.7% of total health insurance premiums. In Colorado, Kaiser has a higher market share for total health insurance premiums than the next two health insurers combined. Rocky Mountain Health Plan and United Healthcare together only comprise 23.4% of total health insurance premiums written.[50]

Full Service Health Plans in California, 2011

Health Plan Name	Enrollee %	Revenue %
Kaiser Foundation Health Plan, Inc.	30.89%	47.01%
Blue Cross of California	14.82%	10.80%
Health Net of California, Inc.	10.30%	9.20%
California Physicians' Service	10.94%	8.10%
UHC of California	3.81%	6.24%
Aetna Health of California, Inc.	3.59%	1.75%
Heritage Provider Network, Inc.	2.05%	1.59%
Scan Health Plan	0.51%	1.57%
Orange County Health Authority	1.93%	1.43%
Local Initiative Health Authority For L.A. County	4.19%	1.33%
Cigna HealthCare of California, Inc.	1.03%	0.92%
Inland Empire Health Plan	2.23%	0.84%
Care 1st Health Plan	1.63%	0.74%
CareMore Health Plan	0.21%	0.70%
Partnership HealthPlan of California	0.74%	0.68%
Santa Cruz-Monterey-Merced Managed Med. Care Comm.	0.94%	0.57%
Molina Healthcare of California	1.58%	0.55%
All Others	8.61%	5.99%
Total	100.00%	100.00%

Kaiser has likely been successful because it is the low-cost provider of healthcare. Employers that are predisposed to choose the low-cost health insurance plan for their employees choose Kaiser. This need to provide low-cost healthcare to be competitive may be driving many other hospitals and health systems to employ physicians in an effort to duplicate the Kaiser model.

Kaiser's closed network HMOs and MCI's cellular networks are strikingly similar innovations. Kaiser's HMOs are relatively small networks of providers within a geographic area. Patients lose the flexibility to choose from thousands of physicians as with preferred provider organizations (PPOs), but they gain great cost and operational efficiencies from the small provider networks.

Similarly, MCI's cellular network model was developed because only a limited number of phone calls could be served on each frequency at the same time, and only a limited number of frequencies were available. MCI's innovation was to develop small geographic cells for each frequency and a switching model that would invisibly move calls from one frequency to another if customers moved around. Because the small cells needed to serve fewer customers at any given time, the cellular network could serve more customers with a limited number of frequencies by alternating a limited number of frequencies geographically in a honeycomb-like grid.

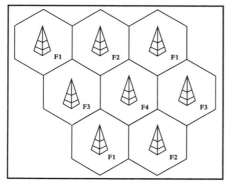

Source: Wiki Commons[51]

Just like Ma Bell, the FTC has challenged multiple hospital mergers and physician practice acquisitions that it deemed would restrict trade and free markets. The following are seven challenges during the last five years:

- 7/24/2009: The FTC issued an administrative complaint challenging Carilion Clinic's 2008 acquisition of two outpatient clinics in the Roanoke, Virginia, area. Prior to the acquisition, the Center for Advanced Imaging (CAI) and the Center for Surgical Excellence (CSE) had strong reputations for offering high-quality care and convenient services at prices much lower than Carilion. The complaint alleged that Carilion's acquisition of these outpatient centers eliminated vital competition in violation of federal antitrust laws and led to higher healthcare costs and reduced incentives to maintain and improve service and quality of care for patients in the Roanoke area.[52] The parties settled in December 2009, and Carilion agreed to divest the two centers to entities approved by the FTC.[53]

- 4/20/2011: The FTC challenged Phoebe Putney Health System, Inc.'s (Phoebe's) proposed acquisition of rival Palmyra Park Hospital, Inc. (Palmyra) from HCA, in Albany, Georgia. The FTC's administrative complaint alleged that the deal would reduce competition significantly and allow the combined Phoebe/Palmyra to raise prices for general acute-care hospital services charged to commercial health plans, substantially harming patients and local employers and employees. The parties settled in August 2013.[54,55]

- 3/28/2012: The FTC ruled that ProMedica Health System's August 2010 acquisition of rival St. Luke's Hospital was anticompetitive and likely to substantially lessen competition and increase prices for general acute-care inpatient hospital services and inpatient obstetric services sold to commercial health plans in the Toledo, Ohio area. In a 4-0 decision, the Commission ordered ProMedica to divest St. Luke's Hospital to an FTC-approved buyer within six months after the Commission order became final and effective.[56]

- 4/13/2012: The FTC dismissed the complaint it issued in November 2011 seeking to block OSF Healthcare System's acquisition of rival healthcare provider Rockford Health System in light of OSF Healthcare's decision to abandon the proposed transaction. The Commission voted 5-0 to dismiss the complaint after OSF announced it would no longer seek to complete the acquisition.[57]

- 8/06/12: Renown Health, the largest provider of acute care hospital services in northern Nevada, released its staff cardiologists from noncompete contract clauses, allowing up to 10 of them to join competing cardiology practices. Renown Health has agreed to settle FTC charges that its recent acquisitions of two local cardiology groups reduced competition for the provision of adult cardiology services in the Reno area. In 2010 and 2011, Renown acquired Sierra Nevada Cardiology Associates (15 cardiologists) and Reno Heart Physicians (16 cardiologists), giving it an 88% market share for cardiology services in the area.[58]

- 11/16/2012: The FTC blocked Reading Health System's proposed acquisition of Surgical Institute of Reading L.P. (SIR), alleging that the combination of the two healthcare providers would substantially reduce competition in the area surrounding Reading, Pennsylvania, and lead to reduced quality and higher healthcare costs for the area's employers and residents. The FTC, jointly with the Pennsylvania Attorney General, filed a complaint in federal district court seeking a preliminary injunction to stop the deal pending an administrative trial.[59]

- 3/12/2013: The FTC and the Idaho Attorney General announced they will file a complaint in federal district court seeking to block St. Luke's Health System, Ltd.'s acquisition of Idaho's largest independent, multispecialty physician practice group, Saltzer Medical Group, P.A. According to the joint complaint, the combination of St. Luke's and Saltzer would give it the market power to demand higher rates for healthcare services provided by primary care physicians (PCPs) in Nampa, Idaho. St. Luke's is a not-for-profit health system with headquarters in Boise, Idaho. It owns and operates six hospitals. Before being acquired by St. Luke's, Saltzer was a for-profit, physician-owned, multispecialty group located in Nampa. With approximately 44 physicians, Saltzer was the largest and oldest independent multispecialty physicians' group in Idaho. Its specialties include family practice, internal medicine, and pediatrics.[60]

INSURANCE CONSOLIDATION

As described at the beginning of this chapter, health insurers have consolidated, just as health systems have. The following chart illustrates the market capitalizations for the largest publicly traded health insurance companies in 2014. In 1995 there were over one dozen publicly traded health insurers. Now five companies comprise 99% of this group. Many would identify United Healthcare as the "big dog" of the market. WellPoint, based in Indianapolis, grew by acquiring Blue Cross Blue Shield health plans in several states. Aetna grew by acquiring U.S. Healthcare and Coventry.

Kaiser, Health Care Services Corporation, and the Mayo Clinic are not publicly traded, but all three are definitely formidable health plans to be sure.

2014 – Top 5 Publicly Traded Health Insurers Comprise 99% of Total Market Capitalization

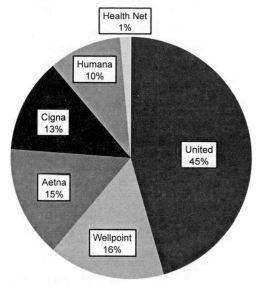

Source: Google Finance, April 2014

HEALTH SYSTEM CONSOLIDATION

Health systems may consolidate by either acquiring different types of healthcare businesses to create "integrated delivery systems" or by acquiring multiple healthcare businesses that do the same thing.

Vertical Consolidation

Integrated delivery systems acquire and develop a wide array of healthcare services to provide for every possible healthcare need of the community. A health system with only one hospital can develop an integrated health system by purchasing or developing services for imaging, surgery, laboratory, rehabilitation, skilled nursing facilities, home health, and long-term care.

Several hundred charitable hospitals have been stressed to the point of failure by decreased reimbursement from Medicare and Medicaid and increased pressure from physician-owned ancillary businesses. The thousands of ambulatory surgery centers, outpatient imaging centers, urgent care centers, dialysis centers, and all the other organizations discussed in this book are all active competitors with hospitals.

Many not-for-profit hospitals have sold out or entered into joint operating arrangements with regional and mega health systems. An important benefit of being part of a mega health system is the improved bond ratings hospitals can achieve by jointly guaranteeing the debt of all the hospitals in their system. Together, many hospitals that agree to guarantee each other's debt are a less risky investment than a single hospital. Bond ratings are important because they determine the interest rates hospitals have to pay bond holders when they need to raise money to build facilities or fund operations. The following is a list of twenty-five of the largest not-for-profit hospital systems in the United States.

Not-for-Profit Mega Health Systems[61]

1. Ascension Health (St. Louis) — 81
2. Catholic Health Initiatives (Denver) — 76
3. Trinity Health (Novi, Mich.) — 49
4. Adventist Health System (Winter Park, Fla.) — 41
5. Dignity Health (San Francisco) — 40
6. Kaiser Foundation Hospitals (Oakland, Calif.) — 36
7. Catholic Health East (Newton Square, Pa.) — 35
8. Sanford Health (Sioux Falls, S.D. and Fargo, N.D.) — 34
9. Carolinas Healthcare System (Charlotte, N.C.) — 33
10. CHRISTUS Health (Irving, Texas) — 32
11. Providence Health System (Seattle) — 32
12. Mercy (Chesterfield, Mo.) — 31

13. Baylor Health Care System (Dallas, Texas) — 30
14. Avera Health (Sioux Falls, S.D.) — 29
15. Iowa Health System (Des Moines) — 26
16. Banner Health (Phoenix) — 25
17. Catholic Healthcare Partners (Cincinnati) — 24
18. Sutter Health (Sacramento, Calif.) — 24
19. Mayo Clinic (Rochester, Minn.) — 23
20. Intermountain Healthcare (Salt Lake City) — 22
21. New York-Presbyterian Healthcare System — 20
22. Adventist Health (Roseville, Calif.). — 19
23. Bon Secours Health System (Marriottsville, Md.) — 19
24. IU Health (Indianapolis) — 17
25. SSM Health Care (St. Louis) — 17

However, health system relationships are just like any other type of relationship. Some do not last. In 2009, The Christ Hospital in Cincinnati finally withdrew from the Health Alliance of Greater Cincinnati after a three-year legal battle.[62] The Christ Hospital was the most profitable hospital in the system and lacked control over the use of its assets. Just prior to The Christ Hospital's withdrawal, the Health Alliance had developed and built a brand new hospital on the north side of Cincinnati.

For-profit hospitals may also acquire or partner with struggling not-for-profit hospitals. Publicly traded hospital chains like Community Health Systems, HCA, Universal Health Services, and Tenet all pursue acquisitions of not-for-profit hospitals.

ANALOGY: THE CATHEDRAL AND THE BAZAAR

Now that we have covered all of the different financial arrangements between physicians and hospitals, we can compare and contrast two opposing business philosophies that hospitals and health systems may use with respect to physician independence and physician employment. I'll refer to these opposing approaches as *the Cathedral* and *the Bazaar,* in honor of Eric Raymond's book by the same title.

The cathedral represents the rigid and authoritarian organization that is massive and powerful but slow to change. The cathedral is organized and lays plans for the next several decades. It is not as adaptive as the bazaar, but over the long term institutional organizations tend to outlast proprietorships and self-employed individuals.

Over the centuries, the church-sponsored hospitals (cathedrals) have led the charge, even before government, in meeting the social needs of the general population. Church-sponsored hospitals provided medical care to the elderly and poor long before Medicare and Medicaid were created. Medicare is now a $600 billion per year industry, comprising 20% of all healthcare dollars spent in the United States, while Medicaid spending is over $400 billion per year. Church-sponsored hospitals had a huge head start in these industries. This is one of the reasons there are still so many church-sponsored hospitals today.

The bazaar refers to the seemingly chaotic marketplace where tradespeople competitively sell the wares of their labor and skill to consumers. I imagine an agora (marketplace) in Greece where farmers, blacksmiths, and artisans set up their tents side-by-side and compete head-to-head for customers. The competition forced the vendors to provide excellent products and service or possibly lose business to the other sellers.

Retailers, the profession of middlemen, were created to rapidly accelerate the growth of the bazaar marketplace. Retailers gave tradespeople the ability to be more productive. The retailers could sit in the marketplace during the day while the tradespeople were elsewhere making their products. This was a huge benefit to the tradespeople because it gave them many more hours during the day to do their specialized work.

In our analogy, the bazaar refers to the marketplace of independent physician practices. The independent physicians are small business owners providing specialized services competitively against other independent physicians. Just like the agora tradespeople, independent physicians employ office support staff to focus on patient scheduling, medical records, billing, answering phones, and taking patients' basic vital information. The support staff enables physicians to focus on providing medical services to patients as much as possible and minimizing the time they devote to the non-medical duties it takes to operate a medical practice.

The requirements of operating a physician practice have changed dramatically over the past 120 years. Whereas physicians used to go from house to house on horseback, only seeing a few patients per day, a family practice physician in an office-based clinic in 2014 may see twelve to twenty patients per day, every day. This level of productivity is a function of the elaborate factory-style physician offices that have developed over the years. If a physician had to answer all the phone calls, check in patients, and complete all paperwork themselves, it would be a challenge to treat more than four or five patients per day.

Despite the structure that independent physician practices have developed to remain competitive, their small structures as small businesses still leave them relatively flexible and responsive compared to large organizations. A small practice can have internal discussions about changing a basic process in the morning and implement that change by the afternoon because there are very few decision makers. The physician owners of the practice can make decisions in an instant.

EXAMPLE: GENERAL HOSPITAL EMBRACES THE BAZAAR

General Hospital is our fictional illustration of a hospital that provides all its services via contractual service arrangements with independent physicians. My experience with over 100 unique hospitals and health systems leads me to believe that General Hospital is fairly representative of one-off community hospitals throughout the United States and major institutions that have purposefully positioned themselves as the destination for independent physician practitioners.

Emergency Department

General Hospital has an emergency department coverage agreement in place with a local group of emergency medicine physicians who also provide coverage at three other hospitals in the region. The emergency physician group is engaged to provide at least two emergency medicine physicians on-site at all times, 24 hours per day, 7 days per week, 365 days per year.

Because the flow of patients is not always even, but at least two physicians must be on-site at all times, there are often slow periods and downtime periods when the physicians are idle. Also, because the physicians are not staying productive, and they cannot leave, the group can't make enough money from insurance collections to cover its physician salaries. Therefore, to support the group's ability to provide the minimum staffing complement, General Hospital pays the group a subsidy in addition to the professional collection the physician group receives directly from insurance companies. The emergency medicine subsidy is about $350,000 per year.

Hospitalist Coverage

General Hospital frequently has patients admitted through the emergency department for inpatient medical care. When the admitted patients do not have a primary care physician, General Hospital, like most hospitals, must provide physicians who can oversee the medical care of these unassigned patients. Additionally, some primary care physicians in the community do not want to round on their patients when they are admitted through the ED or for other reasons. These community physicians may have busy clinical schedules or other duties that make it difficult for them to stop what they're doing and go to the hospital.

General Hospital engages a local internal medicine group to be responsible for all unassigned and emergent inpatients. Four physicians in the internal medicine group take turns rounding on General Hospital's inpatients in the mornings, afternoons, and evenings. The group also engages other community physicians to work on a per-shift basis. These contract physicians assign all insurance payments to the internal medicine group in exchange for flat shift payments.

General Hospital pays the internal medicine group $400,000 per year for rounding on its inpatients and also managing the physician contractors. The group keeps the hospital subsidy and all the insurance payments from treating the hospital patients and pays the various physician contractors for their time.

Radiology

General Hospital has several x-rays, two MRIs, a CT scanner, and two ultrasounds. Collectively, tens of thousands of imaging tests are ordered each year by the emergency department, inpatient unit, ICU, and community physicians. General Hospital employs a team of technologists to operate each machine, but only trained and licensed radiologists are qualified to interpret test results for x-rays, MRIs, CT scans, and ultrasounds.

General Hospital has a radiology coverage arrangement with Radiological Consultants to provide professional interpretations between 7:00 a.m. and 7:00 p.m. each day. During evening hours, the hospital contracts with a teleradiology group to interpret scans remotely. Teleradiology coverage is often referred to as "Night Hawk" coverage.

Because over 50% of the emergency department's imaging is for patients with Medicaid or no insurance, the radiology group is paid a subsidy of $600,000 per year to make up for a lack of payments from insurance companies.

Anesthesiology

About 6,000 surgeries and deliveries are performed in General Hospital's operating rooms each year. Half of these are inpatient surgeries for births and common surgeries like appendix removals, colon resections, hip and knee replacements, hysterectomies, mastectomies, cardiac surgery, and spine surgery. The other half are outpatient surgeries, which might normally be provided in an ambulatory surgery center, but are mostly elderly and high-risk patients for which the surgeons want to have emergency physician backup if needed.

A minority of the surgeries, only a few hundred per year, are emergent in nature. This includes the appendectomies and some trauma surgeries, mostly related to automobile accidents.

General Hospital has eight fully equipped operating rooms with millions of dollars in equipment and instruments. It employs dozens of nurses and techs for pre-op, post-op, and surgery. Over 100 surgeons have been credentialed and granted privileges to perform surgeries there. Many of the surgeons have weekly "block times" reserved for them so they can perform four to six surgeries in a row, bouncing from operating room to operating room.

However, the provision of anesthesia can only be performed by licensed anesthesiologists, who must be present for each and every surgery. General Hospital contracts with Advanced Anesthesiology Group for continuous 24/7 anesthesiology coverage. This requires, each weekday, at least three anesthesiologists on-site between 7:00 a.m. and 4:00 p.m., two anesthesiologists on-site between 4:00 p.m. and 7:00 p.m., and one anesthesiologist on-site from 7:00 p.m. until 7:00 a.m. the next morning. The anesthesiologist on-site in the evenings has relatively little work to do. He (or she) is present primarily for emergent surgeries and deliveries.

Because the evening anesthesiologist coverage does not produce enough insurance payments to cover the $500,000 it costs to staff anesthesiologists at night, General Hospital has to pay the group $350,000 per year to subsidize this coverage.

Intensive Care Coverage: ICU, PICU, NICU

General Hospital is licensed by the state as a Level III trauma center. It has 24 licensed intensive care unit beds, 12 pediatric intensive care beds, and 14 neonatal intensive care beds. The state requires a medical director for each of these departments as well as on-site physician coverage for each area 24 hours per day. This means General Hospital must have critical care intensivist physicians, pediatric intensivists, and neonatologists on-site 24 hours per day, regardless of whether the patient census is 24 beds, 12 beds, or two beds for each department.

As with anesthesiology, there are frequent periods of downtime. Many of the pediatric and neonatal patients are covered by Medicaid or have no insurance at all. As a result, General Hospital has to subsidize the critical care physician group, the pediatric intensivist group, and the neonatology group. Collectively, these three subsidies amount to over $1 million annually.

Specialist On-Call Coverage

While there are always emergency physicians on-site at General Hospital, the emergency physicians do not have the expertise to diagnosis and treat every patient presenting at the emergency department. On a daily basis, they have to call physician specialists for consults. Each hospital maintains a list of physician specialists who are willing to take call coverage and be contacted for emergency department consults. These on-call physicians include OBGYNs, general surgeons, cardiologists, orthopedic surgeons, and a variety of other types of physician specialists.

To procure continuous 24/7 on-call coverage for just these four specialties costs General Hospital over $700,000 per year.

Joint Ventures

General Hospital has four joint ventures with physicians. The first joint venture is a medical office building real estate joint venture with nearly 25 physicians on the hospital campus. Each of the 25 physician groups is an investor in the real estate holding company that owns the building where their offices reside.

The second joint venture is a six-room ambulatory surgery center. General Hospital owns 51% of the surgery center and 31 surgeons own 49% of the surgery center. The primary users of the surgery center are gastroenterologists, ophthalmologists, general surgeons, orthopedic surgeons, urologists, and otolaryngologists (aka, ENTs). The surgery center is a tenant in the medical office building joint venture.

The third joint venture is an MRI center. General Hospital owns 70%, and the radiology group owns 30%. The radiologist group also has the exclusive interpretation contract to read MRIs for the center.

The fourth joint venture is a cath lab joint venture owned by General Hospital (51%) and by a group of 15 cardiologists (49%). The cardiologists perform low-risk catheterizations in an outpatient setting.

Business Services

General Hospital offers an array of business services to independent community physicians. About 120 community physicians contract with General Hospital's MSO for bookkeeping, billing, payroll management, or some combination of these services. Most physicians in the community are also part of the PHO. The PHO performs payor negotiations on behalf of General Hospital and about 280 physicians.

General Hospital's Doctor Deals

<u>The Core Hospital Services</u>

Emergency physician collections guarantee (ED coverage)
Hospitalist collections guarantee (inpatient unit coverage)

<u>Major Support</u>

Radiology CG (interpretation for inpatient, outpatient, consults)
Anesthesiology CG (surgical, delivery, pain coverage)

<u>Intensive Care Coverage</u>

Critical care/intensivist collections guarantee (ICU coverage)
Pediatric intensivist collections guarantee (PICU coverage)
Neonatology collections guarantee (NICU coverage)

<u>Specialist Alignment</u>

OBGYN on-call
OBGYN medical directorship
General surgery & trauma on-call
Surgery medical directorship, chief of surgery
Cardiology on-call
Heart center medical director
Interventional radiology on-call
Orthopedic surgery on-call
Ophthalmology on-call
Plastic surgery on-call
ENT on-call
Podiatry on-call

<u>Advanced Specialist Alignment</u>

Surgery center joint venture
Imaging joint venture
Cath lab joint venture

MOB joint venture

<u>Business Services</u>

Managed care contracting (PHO);
Billing, accounting, payroll services

EXAMPLE: REGIONAL HEALTH SYSTEM: THE CATHEDRAL EMPLOYS PHYSICIANS

Regional Health System is a typical example of a regional hospital system that has embraced physician employment.

Though there are an infinite number of variations of the organization and specialty makeup of the hospital-affiliated physician group, there are two core characteristics of Regional Health System. First, it developed a primary care physician group by recruiting family practice, internal medicine, and pediatricians. Second, it employs inpatient-focused hospitalists who round on its hospital patients instead of relying on independent contractors.

Primary Care

Regional employs over 250 primary care physicians, physician assistants, and nurse practitioners at 40 different clinic locations. These include family practices, internal medicine, pediatrics, occupational health clinics, and urgent care.

These 250 physicians order thousands of tests, make thousands of referrals to specialists, and write thousands of prescriptions. They are Regional's front line for patient referrals. Each physician is required to provide at least three to four days of on-call coverage per month at one or more of its various hospitals.

Emergency Department

Regional has contracts with two different emergency medicine groups. One of the groups provides exclusive coverage at two of its hospitals and the other group provides coverage at the third hospital. Regional pays subsidies for coverage at two of the three hospitals.

Hospitalist Coverage

Regional employs over two dozen full-time hospitalists to round on it inpatients. This saves its primary care physicians a lot of time providing on-call coverage.

Radiology

Regional has contracts with a large radiology group to perform reads for all three hospitals. Because the radiology coverage agreement is so large and there are two large radiology groups in the area, this radiology group agreed to take it without demanding any financial support.

Anesthesiology

Regional has contractually engaged a group for 24/7 coverage. The group does not receive a subsidy or collections guarantee.

Intensive Care Coverage: ICU, PICU, NICU

All PICU and NICU coverage is provided by Regional's employed physicians, but it still contracts with a critical care group for continuous coverage of its adult ICU. Regional does not subsidize its critical care contractor.

Specialist On-Call Coverage

Regional employs a cardiology group, three OBGYN groups, one orthopedic surgeon, a general surgeon group, and various other individual specialists. Each specialist is required to provide four to five days of on-call coverage per month as part of their employment agreement. Regional pays extra *per diem* payments for specialists willing to take additional calls each month.

The specialists perform surgeries at Regional's facilities and order all imaging from Regional's imaging centers.

Joint Ventures

Regional had six joint ventures over the years, but only one joint venture still exists. Regional has a noncompete clause in its physician employment agreements that precludes employed physicians from having investments in businesses that compete with Regional. As a result, Regional gradually bought out all of its physician joint ventures as more and more physician became employed by it and its competitors.

The only joint venture that remains is its imaging center joint venture with the radiology group.

Regional Health System's Doctor Deals

The Foundation - Employed Primary Care (250 providers)

Family practice – (employed physicians)
Internal medicine – (employed physicians)
Pediatricians – (employed physicians)

The Core Hospital Services

Emergency physician contract (ED coverage, two subsidies)
Employed hospitalists (>24 FTEs)

Major Support

Radiology contract (no subsidy)
Anesthesiology contract (no subsidy)

Intensive Care Coverage

Critical care contractor (ICU coverage, no subsidy)
Pediatric intensivists (PICU coverage, employed physicians)
Neonatologists (NICU coverage, employed physicians)

Employed Specialists/Specialist Alignment

OBGYN employees (5 days on-call per employee)
OBGYN medical directorship
General surgery employees (trauma on-call coverage 5 days each)
Surgery medical directorship, chief of surgery
Cardiology employees (on-call 5 days each)
Heart center medical director
Orthopedic surgery employee & contractors (paid call)
Paid call contractors for all other coverage needs

Specialist Alignment

Imaging joint venture

Chapter 7
Deals for the Results We Want

OVERVIEW

This chapter discusses the following topics related to the future of doctor deals:

- Chronic Diseases Drive 75% of Healthcare Costs

- An Extremely Effective and Under-Utilized Treatment

- Contract Deals and Accountable Care

- Health Quality Partners

- Montefiore Medical Center

- Hennepin Health

- Post-Acute Contract Deals

- Medication Adherence Data

- What Doctors Can and Can't Do

- Hearts & Minds

- Treatment Adherence and Patient Behavior Theories

- Treatment Adherence Experts

- Closing Remarks

CHRONIC DISEASES DRIVE 75% OF HEALTHCARE COSTS

As I said in the introduction, the information in *Doctors Deals* can be adapted and applied to solve a lot of the industry's big problems. By far, the single largest problem we have to overcome is to improve the quality, access, and cost of chronic disease care.

Chronic disease is certainly the quintessential healthcare problem of our era. Eighty-four percent of U.S. healthcare spending is on people with chronic diseases,[63] and 75% of U.S. healthcare spending is specifically related to the treatment of chronic diseases.[64] Since we've beaten down the microbial diseases, we're left fighting a long, painful, and expensive war on cardiovascular diseases, diabetes, chronic obstructive pulmonary disease (COPD), and cancer.

Leading Annual Causes of Death in US (2010 CDC)

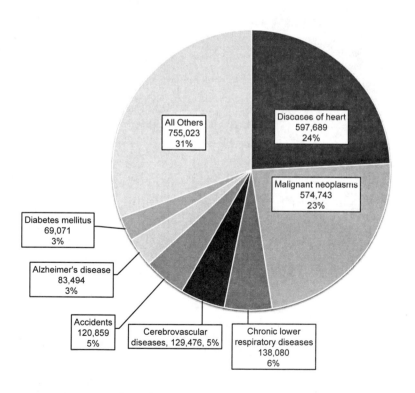

AN EXTREMELY EFFECTIVE AND UNDER-UTILIZED TREATMENT

Congestive heart failure (CHF) is one of the most financially crippling chronic diseases for insurance companies and patients. CHF is the most common reason for Medicare enrollees to be admitted to a hospital, and CHF patients are some of the most expensive of all health insurance enrollees to treat on an ongoing basis. According to the Care Continuum Alliance, the per member per month cost for CHF patients is about $2,700.[65] Over the course of a year, this equates to about $30,000 every year for each CHF patient. By comparison, I scanned a number of health insurance reports for their average per member per month cost and found most of them in the $250 to $300 per month range.

At a basic level, CHF occurs when a person's heart pumps weakly or with a lack of adequate force. This causes fluid to back up in the lungs. CHF patients may feel shortness of breath and fatigue. The normal treatment involves drugs, particularly a water pill, which serves as a diuretic to drain off the excess water being held by the patient's body. I read an example of a recently diagnosed CHF patient who lost fifteen pounds of water in the first three days after he started taking his water pill.

In a CHF mortality study conducted in 2000, 2,445 residents of Worcester, Massachusetts, were followed for five years after initially being identified by discharges from one of 11 hospitals in the area for confirmed acute CHF.[66] Three-fourths of the population had been diagnosed with CHF prior to their hospitalization. The mean age of the study population was 76 years. Among the population, 37% died during the first year after their hospitalization, and 79% died during the five-year follow-up period.

The Framingham Heart Study demonstrated better longevity for women than men.[67] Between 1948 and 1988, the Framingham

---

Heart Study identified 652 participants who developed CHF. The mean age at diagnosis increased markedly from decade to decade, occurring as early as age 57 in the 1950s to age 72 in the 1970s and age 76 in the 1980s. For men, one-year mortality was 43% and five-year mortality was 75%. For women, one-year mortality was 46% and five-year mortality was 62%. The study found that prognosis was better for women and those diagnosed at younger ages. Surprisingly, advances in various types of treatments over the 40-year study period did not translate into better survival rates for patients in more recent decades than those who contracted CHF in the early decades of the study.

While all this sounds pretty bad, CHF is actually very treatable, and the best treatments are extremely affordable. After all, the water pill is just a diuretic. The other treatment, cardiac rehabilitation, is a physician-supervised program that furnishes physician prescribed exercise; cardiac risk factor modification, including education, counseling, and behavioral intervention; psychosocial assessment; and outcomes assessment.

Cardiac rehabilitation is a medically supervised program for patients who have just had a heart attack, cardiac catheterization, CABG or other invasive heart surgery, or angina. Medicare pays for up to 36 cardiac rehab sessions if one of the aforementioned events has occurred in the past 12 months.

The core exercise component of cardiac rehab is really just walking on a treadmill and or riding a stationary bicycle. In a hospital setting, Medicare pays about $100 for every session of cardiac rehab. According to Medicare, it paid for about 2.6 million sessions of cardiac rehab during a recent year. If cardiac rehab is conducted in a physician's office, the reimbursement is $17 to $25 per session.

Cardiac rehab is arguable one of the most cost effective treatments available. A 2004 meta-analysis of 81 studies, including 30 randomized control trials, demonstrated that cardiac rehab is definitely safe.[68] In 60,000 hours of patient exercise, there were no adverse events reported. This means no one had another heart attack during their bouts of exercise. This meta-analysis demonstrated that the odds ratio for mortality, that is, death, was 0.71. Therefore, for the various studies included in this meta-analysis, the odds of dying were 29% lower for exercising participants than non-exercising participants. This odds ratio had a *p value* of 0.06. This means that there was only a 6% chance that the difference in mortality between the exercise groups and non-exercise groups was due to chance alone.

A single, more vivid study from the 1990s took 100 CHF patients and put half in an exercise group that closely resembled the coverage benefit for Medicare's cardiac rehab benefits. The exercise group underwent low-intensity aerobics three times a week for eight weeks and then twice per week for one year. At two months, the exercise group demonstrated 18% improvement in aerobic capacity and similar improvements in quality of life. For the exercise group, the relative risk of death was 0.37 compared to the non-exercise group, or 63% lower. The relative risk of hospital readmission for heart failure was 0.29, or 71% lower than the non-exercise group. There was less than a 2% chance that the differences between the two groups were caused by chance.

Despite compelling evidence of the benefits and the affordability of cardiac rehab, treatment adherence is stunningly low. Medicare data indicates that cardiac rehab is only used by 14% of eligible patients following heart attacks and 31% of patients following CABG surgery.[69] The most commonly cited barriers include distance from the program facility; transportation; low patient self-esteem; and lack of physician referral, perceived benefit, and social support.[70]

In 2009, CMS noted the lack of evidence on the effect of cardiac rehabilitation on health outcomes in Medicare beneficiaries with CHF. Ongoing research since the last review has provided sufficient evidence for reconsideration. The American Association of Cardiovascular and Pulmonary Rehabilitation (AACVPR), American College of Cardiology (ACC), American Heart Association (AHA), and the Heart Failure Society of America (HFSA) submitted a formal request for a National Coverage Determination to add CHF to the list of approved indications for coverage for cardiac rehabilitation.

In November 2013, the Centers for Medicare and Medicaid Services (CMS) proposed to cover cardiac rehabilitation for CHF patients.[71] During the initial 30-day comment period, almost all of the 182 comments favored adding CHF to the list of approved indications for coverage for cardiac rehabilitation. CMS finally announced in February 2014 that it would cover cardiac rehabilitation for CHF.

Currently, cardiac rehabilitation coverage is permitted for Medicare beneficiaries who have experienced one or more of the following:

- An acute myocardial infarction within the preceding 12 months

- A coronary artery bypass surgery

- Current stable angina pectoris

- Heart valve repair or replacement

- Percutaneous transluminal coronary angioplasty (PTCA) or coronary stenting

- A heart or heart–lung transplant

- Chronic heart failure with left ventricular ejection fraction of 35% or less and New York Heart Association class II to IV symptoms despite being on optimal heart failure therapy for at least six weeks

Cardiac rehab is probably one of the most cost-effective medical treatments that is available, and there needs to be more doctor deals to support its use.

Because cardiac rehab qualifies as a designated health service under the Stark Laws, physicians can only own cardiac rehab businesses under the in-office ancillary exception. Therefore, physicians such as cardiologists can self-refer their own patients to cardiac rehab that is wholly self-contained in their own practice. These in-office cardiac rehab businesses cannot accept cardiac rehab referrals from other cardiologists unless the patient changes cardiologists entirely through a patient referral.

So unlike ASCs, which are not designated health services, health systems cannot develop cardiac rehab facilities and then invite cardiologists or cardiac surgeons to invest in them.

The economics of the cardiac rehab business do not align with physicians' economic incentives. As I said before, regular cardiac rehab performed in a hospital setting is reimbursed about $100 per session while the same session in a physician office is reimbursed $17 to $25.

Under Medicare's current fee-for-service reimbursement rates of $20 per session, I do not believe cardiac rehab in a physician office setting is an attractive business for physicians. There are opportunities here for three different types of doctor deals.

First, hospital-based billing doesn't necessarily require that services be provided inside the hospital's main facility. Medicare usually allows hospital-based businesses to be located within 35 miles of the main facility and still be billed under hospital rates. So ideally, a hospital-based cardiac rehab business could be located in a separate suite of the same medical office building where the physicians have their offices. This lends well to medical directorships, rental lease agreements, shared supervisors, management agreements, and clinical co-management.

The second option applies to cardiac rehab provided in Accountable Care Organizations. Under ACO reimbursement, there is fee-for-service payment and an effective bonus based on per member per month costs. In this model there are legal waivers protecting ACOs and their affiliates from violating the Anti-Kickback Statute. With these protections, and the incentive to keep costs as low as possible, it makes good financial sense for the ACO as a whole to provide physicians some sort of subsidy or shared savings distribution that creates a reasonable level of income commensurate to the admissions prevented as a result of cardiac rehab businesses.

This is commercially reasonable because the same service can be provided at a lower cost in a physician office, and the ACO, as a whole, is entitled to 50% to 60% of the shared savings it generates for Medicare. The distribution of these shared savings by the ACO to its affiliate providers are legally waived from risk under the Anti-Kickback Statute.

The third option relates to performance-based clinical management. Because cardiac rehab saves ACOs and hospitals so much money on reduced admission costs, under a performance-based management agreement there is probably a reasonable basis for compensating these physicians more than what they would have earned through an hourly medical director fee. Ideally, this would be predicated on some type of performance incentive.

For example, let's assume a cardiologist would normally be paid $250 per hour for a cardiac rehab medical directorship. Under a performance based contract, the cardiologists may be responsible for all care of patients with heart disease, including cardiac rehab. Under this agreement, it makes sense to incentive the cardiologists to reduce hospital readmissions. If a hospital incurs fewer readmission penalties under traditional FFS Medicare payments, or an ACO realizes shared savings income as a result of reduced readmissions, then it makes sense to pay for the realization of that improvement. This results-based approach could very likely result in an effective rate that is higher than a $250 per hour medical director fee.

CONTRACT DEALS AND ACCOUNTABLE CARE

Medical and non-medical services, for which there is no insurance benefit coverage, are demonstrating high effectiveness in reducing medical costs from chronic diseases. Yet I am disappointed to find that many ACOs are not funding efficacious treatments to contracted affiliate providers in their ACO networks but instead taking the stance that it is patients' responsibility to pay for services when there is no FFS insurance payment.

The whole idea beyond accountable care is to shift away from FFS to make ACOs *accountable* for the ultimate health of the patient. It is no longer about performing a specific emergency room service for a specific dollar amount. It is about proactively getting out in front of diseases and preventing the ED visits and hospitalization from even happening.

If health systems continue to function like they did before they became ACOs, then there is no reason to believe that they will achieve different outcomes as an ACO.

I will discuss three prominent examples of organizations that have achieved exceptional outcomes because they have progressed beyond FFS payment. These examples are Health Quality Partners in Pennsylvania, Montefiore Medical Center in New York, and Hennepin Health in Minneapolis.

HEALTH QUALITY PARTNERS

In 2002, Medicare awarded funding to 15 organizations in the Medicare Coordinated Care Demonstration (MCCD) project to assess whether care coordination programs (e.g., disease management programs) reduced hospitalizations and Medicare expenditures and whether they improved the quality of care for chronically ill Medicare beneficiaries. Randomized clinical trials assigned 18,309 Medicare patients to control and experiment groups for each of the 15 participating organizations.

Of all the participants, only two organizations produced meaningful successful results.[72] These were Mercy Medical Center in Mason City, Iowa, and Health Quality Partners (HQP) in Doylestown, Pennsylvania. HQP has been lauded as the fountain of youth by reducing Medicare hospitalizations by 33% and cutting Medicare costs by 22%. The researchers found five noteworthy differences in these two organizations that separated them from the others.

First, the two successful programs average one in-person nurse visit per patient per month. This was much higher than the average 0.3 in-person visits for the unsuccessful programs. The "in your face" factor created by sending nurses to patients homes appears to be highly effective. According to Randall Brown, a senior fellow at Mathematica Policy Research, the outside research organization that was responsible for the randomized trial, and Jeffrey Brenner, founder of the Camden Coalition of Healthcare Providers, these in-person visits make all the difference.[73] Many disease management companies work on a traditional call center model, with nurses contacting patients by telephone. Both men say that the nurse call center model just doesn't work. Real patient behavior modification can't be achieved over a telephone call.

Second, these two programs were most effective at reducing costs for the most severe and costly patients, whereas the vast majority of the unsuccessful programs did not enroll these types of costly patients. This suggests that patient selection is critical in disease management from a cost-effectiveness perspective. The most severe patients are the ones who are most likely to incur a hospitalization in the next year. If a patient is not at risk for a hospital admission in the next year, then the cost of disease management services may not be adequately justified because there is not much opportunity for savings.

Third, for these organizations the treatment groups were significantly more likely than control group members to *report* being taught how to take their medications. Something in the Mercy and HQP program, possibly the in-person meetings, reinforced patients' recollection of medication education.

Fourth, care coordinators for Mercy and HQP collaborated with local hospitals. These hospitals provided their programs with information on patient hospitalizations. This information may have helped identify high risks for readmissions and managing transitions.

Lastly, care coordinators in both programs had the opportunity to get more face time with the patients' physicians. HQP's care coordinators had office space in many of their patients' physician practices to meet with the patients before or after their physician office visits. Mercy frequently met with their patients at the time of their primary care physician appointments. Both programs assigned all of a particular physician's patient participants to single care coordinators, providing a single point of contact for their practice. Only two of the unsuccessful programs also provided office space in physician practices and assigned a single care coordinator to each physician's patients.

HQP has developed a highly effective program. Sadly, the feedback from Medicare seems to be negative. Because HQP is the single organization that has survived out of the original 15 participants, the project has been deemed to not be scalable.

There are great opportunities for businesses like HQP that can reduce hospital readmissions. The takeaways I extracted from this experiment were that HQP focused on the sickest patients with chronic diseases and that they averaged one home visit per month.

Medicare currently does not have a home health benefit for chronically ill patients. Medicare does have a home health benefit for acutely ill homebound patients who are physically incapable of leaving their homes. The Medicare home health benefit is usually used for patients who have been recently discharged from a hospital and need some type of nursing and therapy for two to four months after going home from the hospital.

However, patients who are discharged from a hospital for heart attack, stroke, cardiac cath, or diabetic shock, or similar chronic disease incident, are usually fairly functional. If they don't meet the homebound requirement, they are not eligible for home health.

This is where the industry tends to lose traction on post-acute care and readmissions. When there is no FFS payment coverage from Medicare, or any other payor, nobody wants to pay the bill. The patient will elect not to receive care rather than pay the bill, and hospitals, which are subject to readmission payment penalties, don't want to pay for post-acute care that might not work.

The result? We have terrible readmission rates for chronic disease patients. This phenomenon is not restricted to the United States, either.

According to a 2013 article in *The Telegram* in New Brunswick,[74] 10 eastern Canadian provinces are coordinating an attempt to ease the chronic disease burden on local acute care hospitals.

According to the Eastern Health CEO, widespread smoking,

inactive lifestyles, and obesity are overburdening local hospitals with high readmission rates. The CEO's hospitals will attempt to coordinate preventive community resources for patients who have been admitted to their acute care hospitals five times or more during the past year. At a collaborative meeting of the 10 Canadian provinces, representatives proposed developing home health programs to ease the burden on hospitals as well as training paramedics to provide home visits.

I've heard about, but I haven't seen, any hospitals or ACOs actually paying home health providers to visit non-homebound patients. I understand why. You can spend a lot of money on home visits and still have readmissions. HQP is the case in point. They were the only organization out of 15 that was able to create a cost-effective model that saves more money on patient care than it costs to operate.

Twelve years later, HQP continues to make headlines and will hopefully grow and license its program into other markets outside of Pennsylvania.

MONTEFIORE MEDICAL CENTER

Montefiore affected significant improvements in hospitalization rates, readmission rates, overall expenses, and biometrics for patients with diabetes, asthma, and congestive heart failure (CHF).[75]

To give you a sample, Montefiore reduced inpatient admissions 25% for diabetes patients and 28% for Medicare patients with diabetes. ED visits for patients with CHF decreased 10% from 550 per 1,000 patients to 500 per 1,000 patients. Total healthcare expenses decreased 7% from 2007 to 2010 compared to aggregate healthcare growth of 16% during the same period.

You can read all the details on their improvements in the Agency for Healthcare Research and Quality (AHRQ) report, "Medical Center Establishes Infrastructure to Manage Care Under Capitated Contracts, Leading to Better Chronic Care Management and Lower Utilization and Costs."[75]

The Care Management Company of Montefiore provides care coordination and chronic care management, with insurers covering about 140,000 lives.

The Montefiore Medical House Calls Program provides primary care for the elderly and includes psychosocial support. In-home services include physical exams, preventive screenings, medical tests, medication reconciliation, telemonitoring, and psychiatric care.

Montefiore operates a world-class disease management program with customized software that stratifies and prioritizes high-risk patients. Montefiore maintains disease-specific chronic care protocols, individual care plans, care variation reports, and performance reports comparing physician-specific outcomes for groups of patients with specific conditions.

But the important thing to note is that Montefiore has made major ongoing investments in activities to achieve these clinical outcomes. It has moved beyond the FFS mind-set into population health management.

HENNEPIN HEALTH

Hennepin Health in Minnesota has even applied the ACO model to a Medicaid population.[76] Up to 60% of Hennepin's Medicaid population has substance abuse or mental health needs. Nearly one-third have unstable housing and 30% have more than one chronic disease. Hennepin's care model extends far outside hospital walls into homeless shelters, the county jail, the local health department, and behavioral health providers. Just like

Montefiore, Hennepin has moved beyond FFS payments for services and become entirely accountable for their patients' care, inside and outside the hospital walls.

POST-ACUTE CONTRACT DEALS

CMS announced early in 2014 that 232 acute care hospitals, skilled nursing homes, physician group practices, long-term care hospitals, and home health agencies have entered into agreements to participate in the Bundled Payments for Care Improvement initiative to bundle payments for inpatient hospital services and post-acute medical care. Bundling payment is one way to encourage physicians, hospitals, and other healthcare providers to work together to better coordinate care for patients, both when they are in the hospital and after they are discharged.

Home health, skilled nursing facilities, and primary care physicians are critical providers in post-acute medical care. Yet virtually all clinical management programs and co-management programs to date have been with medical specialists like cardiologists, orthopedists, and surgeons for inpatient and acute outpatient hospital services.

This is partly a practical issue. Procedures, like surgery, are predicated on checklists and protocols. The Surgical Care Improvement Project (SCIP) metrics are specific and actionable tasks that can be tracked for performance measurement. Home health, behavioral health, and primary care are more fluid than surgical services. Primary care and behavioral health, in particular, are vast seas of vague unrelated symptoms. Just getting a correct diagnosis is a good start.

What is troubling about clinical co-management deals is that nearly all of them compensate surgeons and cardiologists for quality inpatient services, but there are very few formal programs that focus on preventing hospital admissions and readmissions. I have encountered a few.

1. Project RED: Researchers at the Boston University Medical Center (BUMC) developed and tested the Re-Engineered Discharge (RED). Research showed that the RED was effective at reducing readmissions and post-hospital ED visits. The Agency for Healthcare Research and Quality contracted with BUMC to develop a toolkit to assist hospitals, particularly those that serve diverse populations, to replicate the RED.

2. Project BOOST: Project BOOST is a national initiative led by the Society of Hospital Medicine to improve the care of patients as they transition from hospital to home. A study of 11 hospitals that implemented one or more Project BOOST tools published online in the Journal of Hospital Medicine indicated that hospitals implementing Project BOOST experienced a reduction in 30-day readmissions by an average of 13.6%.

3. Intensive Cardiac Rehabilitation (ICR) Programs: ICR programs are lifestyle behavior modification programs that are funded by Medicare after CMS has reviewed and approved scientific evidence that each program is effective through the National Coverage Determination process. The Dr. Ornish Program for Heart Disease Reversal and the Pritikin Program are the only two ICR programs approved as of this book's publication. The Benson-Henry Institute Cardiac Wellness Program will likely be the third ICR program approved.

Post-acute doctor deals for physician-led management of hospital discharges are great opportunities to reduce hospital readmissions through the emergency department. HQP, Montefiore, and Hennepin's successes all relate, in part, to primary care and post-acute management of non-hospital, high-risk patients. Often home visits by nurses, therapists, or aides are a component of these programs.

Patient adherence to physician-prescribed regimens for medications, therapies, physical activity, diet, and health behaviors (e.g., smoking and alcohol consumption) are predictive of hospital readmissions. Patients generally self-manage many elements of these regimens without direct supervision of medical providers. Post-acute services allow physicians to continuously monitor their patients' adherence to prescribed regimens.

As with all performance-based arrangements, it is important to pick the right metrics when developing a management arrangement for post-acute services. Fortunately, patient adherence is an established field, and the metrics and tools for assessing patient adherence to prescribed medical treatments are numerous.

MEDICATION ADHERENCE DATA

Treatment adherence to medication, diet, and exercise regimens is core to chronic disease management. Yet even medication adherence, arguable the easiest of these three components is poor. Getting patients to perform the relatively simple act of continually taking prescribed medications in the correct dosage and frequency is astonishingly difficult to accomplish.

A 2008 meta-analysis of 139 studies found that non-compliance with medication treatments for cardiovascular diseases and diabetes is a real problem.[77] Overall, patients participating in the studies were not taking their medication about 30% of days during treatment. Looking at the data another way, 41% of patients were found to take their medications less than 80% of the days they should be taken.

If adherence to popping a pill is this bad, imagine how poor adherence is for exercise and dietary regimens that require significant motivation, drive, and self-control.

One study estimated that poor medication adherence, by itself, may account for up to $289 billion in U.S. healthcare costs per year, or approximately 13% of U.S. healthcare costs at the time.[78] It is logical that people who take their medication correctly would be healthier, and the implication is that if we could get everyone to take their medicines on time in the right dosages, we could cut 10% to 13% of the nation's healthcare costs pretty easily. However, forward-looking experimental tests to compare the health of medication-adherent patients and medication–non-adherent patients have been very unsuccessful.

A clinical science discussion follows, but I believe it is important for attorneys and business people to know this information, because you don't want to spend a lot of time and money putting together deals and selecting performance metrics that don't drive the desired results.

Regression is a powerful statistical tool for explaining relationships retrospectively. You can take a data set of behaviors and develop a formula to explain the outcomes, just like the ones you learned in high school algebra or college statistics. For example

$$y = mx + b$$

outcome = factor times variable + constant

or in a sophisticated multivariable formula, this may look like

risk of heart disease = $ax1 + bx2 + cx3 + dx4 + e$

The limitation of regression is that you can only test your formula's ability to predict the past. To see if the cause-and-effect relationship truly exists, you have to do a randomized controlled trial (RCT). An RCT sets up a test group and a control group and tests the hypothesis prospectively by giving one group the intervention and not the other. The object of the prospective experiment is to see if a given intervention will drive the predicted outcome in the real world. It is one thing to find an explanatory formula that can describe what has already happened. It is another to see if that formula can predict the future. A formula that can explain the past cannot necessarily predict the future.

The importance of the RCT is critical to the discussion of medication adherence because there are plenty of retrospective regression analyses that demonstrate a strong correlation between medication adherence and positive health outcomes and cost savings. Oddly enough, though, the majority of RCTs have not been successful in affecting medication adherence or ultimate health outcomes.

In an attempt to assess interventions to improve medication adherence, the AHRQ narrowed a list of over 3,900 research articles down to just 68 articles.[79] Of these, 64 articles were for RCTs. Despite a wide range of different types of interventions and diseases, only three of the RCTs even demonstrated "moderate" strength of evidence that the interventions were effective in influencing medication adherence, and these were only for specific diseases. All of the other trials only indicated low strength of evidence or insufficient evidence for improving medication adherence. Further, only a few of the RCTs demonstrated that achieving medication adherence resulted in improved health outcomes or other important end results.

The AHRQ's review is particularly depressing. While we have retrospectively observed that there is a significant cost difference between patients who do and don't take their medications correctly, only three RCTs were able to create even moderate medication adherence, and only one of those three demonstrated a moderate effect of medication adherence on improving health outcomes.

We can't really explain this, or more accurately, we can't explain it very well. However, these studies are important, because we've identified nearly five dozen intervention–disease combinations that we now know are largely ineffective in getting patients to take their medications correctly. Numerous experiments have dug deeper to study the predictors of medication adherence. All of these studies have acknowledged that medication adherence is a complex problem attributed to multiple factors.

An important distinguishing factor to consider in reviewing medication adherence literature is how patient medication adherence is measured. Self-reported adherence, in which the patient self-identifies how often he or she takes medication on time and in the correct dosage, is probably not the best measure. Moreover, in real-world practices, physicians are relying on patient self-management for medication with less than stellar results. Over 40 U.S. states have active narcotics monitoring systems for the specific purpose of preventing the resale and abuse of pain killers. In these states, physicians suspecting patients may be drug abusers can check their state's database to see if other physicians have prescribed their patients narcotics as well as where, when, and how often these patients refill their prescriptions.

Unfortunately, prescription drug dispensing monitoring has been primarily confined to abused narcotics. Though physicians commonly order prescriptions through electronic medical record systems that directly submit the prescription to patients' pharmacies electronically, the electronic prescribing record is often not mapped to the dispensing record so physicians can calculate if patients are refilling their prescriptions on time for statins, beta blockers, insulin, and other medicines for chronic diseases. If a 30-day prescription is refilled twice over a 120-day period, this implies that the patient only used their medicines on 90 of the 120 days for a treatment day-adherence rate of 75%. Even if patient medical records and pharmacy dispensing records are electronically connected so that this statistic can be calculated, dispensing statistics are not considered to be the end all measurement of medication adherence by themselves. Patients could be refilling their prescriptions at 30 days, even if they have skipped days and have unused doses. Alternatively, patients could be over-medicating themselves, running out early, and refilling their prescription on time.

One advance in medication monitoring technology is the invention of electronic medication bottle caps that monitor the date and time when the bottle is opened. Some caps report the last date and time the bottle was opened directly on a digital display on the bottle cap to help patients remember. Some electronic caps also have the ability to electronically send the use data to the medical provider for review. If the electronic record shows that a patient only opened their medication bottle 17 times during a 30-day period, then the patient's physician will have reason to believe that the patient forgot to take their medicine about 43% of treatment days. Ideally, this data could then be corroborated by the dispensing record, which should be 13 days late.

The research related to electronic medical caps is promising. A 1992 study of hypertensive patients found that those with electronic caps that digitally showed them the last time they took their medication on the lid achieved a 95% adherence rate compared to the control group at 78%.[80] The intervention group also showed improvements in blood pressure, while the control group did not.

There was a meta-analysis performed on the effectiveness of electronic medication monitoring for 79 clinical trials between 1995 and 2011.[81] However, there may be significant publishing bias as the paper's sponsor was Aardex Group, a manufacturer of electronic medication caps. Taking this into account, the review of the 79 clinical trials indicates that medication adherence was 74% in the intervention groups, compared to 60% in the control groups. Additionally, 48 of the studies included some form of adherence feedback in which each patient's adherence performance was specifically shared with them. For this subset of studies, the improvement in medication adherence was nearly 20% over the control group.

Here's the really odd thing, though. This meta-analysis of electronic medication monitoring demonstrated real improvements in medication adherence. However, like the AHRQ meta-analysis, very few of these studies translated into improvements in health outcomes. Of the 57 medication studies reviewed using electronic monitoring, only eight reported significant improvements in health outcomes. So while electronic medication caps are demonstrated to probably be the most effective means of improving medication adherence, this adherence only translated into evidence for improved health in eight out of 57 studies in the Aardex Group's meta-analysis and three studies in the AHRQ's meta-analysis.

I couldn't believe these results when I first saw them in the AHRQ review, but the more I read, the more convincing the evidence became. The Aardex Group study sealed the deal for me because it was actually sponsored by the people who manufacture the bottle caps. If even they are admitting that medication adherence doesn't translate into meaningful improvements in health, then I'm highly inclined to believe them. They have a lot to gain by saying taking your drugs improves your health, and their findings indicate a weak correlation.

The poor relationship in outcomes from the AHRQ and Aardex studies of medication adherence can be partially explained by a 2002 meta-analysis of 63 studies of treatment adherence for several types of diseases and treatments. For all types of diseases and treatments studied, including both medication treatments and non-medication treatments, the relative risk ratio of adherence versus non-adherence was 26%.

Relative risk ratio is an obscure measurement to non-researchers, so it requires some explanation. In simplest terms, this means that the relationship between treatment adherence for any one type of treatment does not have a direct one-to-one relationship with health outcomes. Some perfectly adherent patients will not improve and some non-adherent patients will get better while not adhering to their treatment at all. The relative risk ratio helps us to measure the improvement effect of treatment adherence, in spite of the expected randomness of normal outcomes.

A relative risk ratio of 26% means that for a sample of 100 adherent patients, on average 63 patients can be expected to have a good health outcome, while 37 can be expected to have a poor outcome. If adherence had no effect, then we would expect there to be 50 good outcomes and 50 bad outcomes. The overall deviation from the 50–50 split is a 26-point difference. Another ratio, the odds ratio, calculates from this meta-analysis that the odds of having a good outcome are nearly three times higher for patients who are adherent to their treatments.

When we subgroup the 63 studies in this meta-analysis, there are three very exciting findings for chronic disease patients.

First, the relative risk difference is much higher for chronic disease patients than acute disease patients (31% versus 20%). This means that adherence to chronic disease treatments is comparatively more effective than acute disease treatments. If 100 chronic disease patients are adherent to their treatments, we would expect 66 of the patients to have a good outcome and only 33 patients to have a bad outcome.

Second, the relative risk difference is even higher for non-medication treatments than medication treatments (37% versus 21%). If 100 patients are adherent to their non-medication treatments, we would expect 69 patients to have a good outcome and only 31 patients to have a bad outcome.

Third, the relative risk differences were the highest for studies that measure adherence on a continuous scale rather than dichotomous, pass-fail scale (34% versus 13%). This factor demonstrates the strongest difference of the three subgroups identified here. The continuous scale of adherence measurement has been identified as a superior form of measurement in several studies of patient adherence.

These findings are all very good for chronic disease patients Chronic disease treatment adherence has better outcomes than acute disease treatments, non-medication treatment adherence is more effective than medication adherence, and adherence measurement on a continuous scale correlates with better outcomes than rigid pass–fail adherent scores. In addition, most studies only examine the relationship between one adherence factor and a health outcome, such as medication adherence, but not a combination of medication adherence, exercise, and dietary modifications.

As stated before, treatment adherence for chronic disease management is a complex, multifaceted issue. Chronic diseases don't have single, silver-bullet solutions like the antibiotics or vaccines used in acute, infectious disease treatments. While close to 40% of patients may take prescribed medications incorrectly,[82] medication adherence alone is not the silver-bullet solution. Adherence failure rates are almost twice as poor for dietary, exercise, alcohol abuse, and smoking.[83,84,85]

WHAT DOCTORS CAN AND CAN'T DO

This chapter is about using doctor deals to fight chronic disease. Most of the discussion up to this point has been focused on treating chronic disease patients from a post-acute perspective. For example, we have identified great opportunities for improving clinical outcomes for patients with cardiovascular diseases after they have been discharged from a hospital by improving the use of cardiac rehab, implementing chronic disease management programs, and using advances in medication adherence technology. ACOs, the Bundled Payment for Care Improvement initiative, the Hospital Readmission Reduction Program, and the Medicare Coordinated Care Demonstration all focus on improving quality, access, and costs for high-risk patients who are already sick.

The rest of this chapter explores pre-acute medicine and the really tough question: Realistically, how do we prevent chronic disease patients from getting admitted to hospitals in the first place? How do we get patients to adhere to their prescribed lifestyle behavior modifications?

When insufficiencies in reimbursement systems prohibit the provision of necessary services such as anesthesiology, radiology, or emergency medicine, hospitals and health systems traditionally enter into collection guarantees and subsidies, as discussed in Chapter 4, "Contract Deals." The purposes of these arrangements is to ensure the availability and continuity of necessary medical services, above and beyond what reimbursement systems and the economics of each situation. These subsidies ensure access to medical services.

This same idea can be applied to other services. This might include the need for general surgeons in a rural market that otherwise might not be able to support their presence.

This suggests two questions: "What other types of services could be subsidized to improve the health of a population?" and "What factors are prohibiting or inhibiting physicians?"

Certainly physicians have the highest level of didactic and hands-on training in the inner workings of human anatomy. They are the most qualified professionals for diagnosing whether a person has an acute disease or a chronic disease, developing medical and surgical treatment plans, and prescribing safe and effective therapies and medications.

Physicians can freely access all the best diagnostic tools and technology, including basic metabolic panels, complete blood counts, hemoglobin A1C (for diabetes), lipid panels (for cholesterol), c-reactive protein (CRP for arterial inflammation), troponin (test for recent heart attack), prostate-specific androgen (PSA), thyroid stimulating hormone (TSH), pap smears, MRIs, CT scans, echocardiograms, nuclear cardiac stress tests, and electrocardiograms. Lay people don't have access to any of these tests except through their physicians.

Physicians are the gatekeepers for a large number of invaluable prescription medications, from the simple water pill for heart failure to cholesterol-lowering statins; beta blockers, ACE inhibitors, and calcium channel blockers for hypertension; Metformin, Glipizide, Glimepiride, and insulin for diabetes; and blood-thinning antiplatelet drugs to prevent strokes and heart attacks. These drugs have saved millions of lives.

As we all know by now, despite these fantastic tools and medication therapies at physicians' disposal, chronic disease rages on.

So what can't physicians do? And how do these limitations inhibit our success in the war on chronic disease? Generally speaking:

- Physicians can't have long appointments with patients.

- Physicians can't see the same patients every day.

- Physicians can't make patients take their medications on time or in the correct dosages.

- Physicians can't go to the grocery store with patients to make sure they are buying healthy foods and not buying unhealthy foods.

- Physicians can't make patients exercise.

- Physicians can't make patients walk, ride a bicycle, or go to a gym.

- Physicians can't make patients turn off their televisions or computers.

- Physicians can't do house calls.

In my experience, very few physicians, outside of psychiatrists, have the inclination to dedicate time to try to change patients' behavioral issues when they are barriers to treatment adherence. If a patient is non-compliant with a treatment plan, then it must be a psychosomatic issue. Several physicians have authored books with various stories illustrating this tendency. *How Doctors Think*, *What Doctors Feel*, *Intern*, *God's Hotel*, and *County* are all books written by physicians with frustrating stories about alcoholics, drug addicts, and other patients who engage in unhealthy lifestyle behaviors.

In *God's Hotel*, the author speculates that the CEO of her own hospital was killed by a heart attack as a direct result of the stress that his job put on his lifestyle. Can you imagine? A hospital CEO is as far inside the acute medical care system as a non-medical layperson can get. How in the world could such a person die of a heart attack while being constantly surrounded by so many health-oriented cues?

In *What Doctors Feel*, Danielle Ofri, M.D. describes how a patient presented in her office with a laundry list of 30 different symptoms. You can imagine such a list would include nearly every symptom a person could possibly experience. This might include headaches, body aches, back pain, indigestion, fatigue, nausea, chest pain, shortness of breath, anxiety, insomnia, and so on. When asked to rate each symptom in terms of their severity, such a patient assigns every symptom a 10 out of 10.

The author, an internal medicine physician, finds it incredibly difficult to identify any single disease in such a sea of vague, unrelated symptoms, and she only has 20 minutes to do a complete history and physical examination. The waiting room is full of patients, and she can't spend hours with one patient at the expense of all the rest of them. The patient's stress and anxiety seem to be related to constantly taking care of her elderly mother, so her physician prescribes a sleep aid and refers her to a psychiatrist to work through her anxiety.

Several days later Dr. Ofri is called by a hospital emergency department to notify her that this patient has been admitted with pulmonary embolisms (blood clots) in both lungs. This is a serious condition that can kill a person instantly with little or no warning. There was almost no way that Dr. Ofri could have determined this patient had pulmonary embolisms based on her laundry list of symptoms. She could have had several dozen diseases. The sheer volume of symptoms was so overwhelming that they diminished the perceived seriousness of any single one or two.

Dr. Ofri's example is just one of several time-consuming patient archetypes. Others include patients seeking physician approval for disability benefits, those seeking repeated refills for pain narcotics, alcohol and substance abusers, physically abused patients, patients who don't speak English or are deaf, and those do speak English but who just keep talking and talking and talking and never stop.

Psychiatry, the specialty of medicine focused on behavioral health, is unique among the other specialties.

Dr. Sandeep Jauhar, a cardiologist, wrote that he was trying to decide between internal medicine and psychiatry during his third year of medical school. His medical school professors openly expressed disdain for psychiatrists, and his mentor advised him to select internal medicine over psychiatry because it would close the fewest doors. Dr. Jauhar's mentor further informed him that psychiatry was selected by those at the bottom of the medical school class who couldn't get a prestigious residency and those at the top of the class who were mentally ill.

Indeed, other sources cite psychiatry as uniquely separate from the rest of medicine. In the introduction to his book, *How Doctors Think*, Dr. Jerome Groopman asserts that his analysis of physicians' cognitive processes does not apply to physicians in the fields of psychiatry or behavioral health because these disciplines are too broad and complex. I find this ironic because it implies that the thought processes and cognitive abilities of medical and surgical physicians are comparatively simpler and less complex than psychiatrists.

Later in his book, Dr. Groopman cites the story of Myron Fulchuk, M.D., a gastroenterologist in Boston, who repeatedly finds himself trying to discern if the nature of his patients' symptoms are in fact psychiatric. According to Dr. Fulchuk, two patients presented with the same irritable bowel symptoms. One is likely is likely a celiac disease patient, whose digestive system has lost the ability to process gluten. The other patient, with the same symptoms, is hiding the fact that she is self-administering laxatives, which is the real cause of her symptoms. The first patient has a disease of the digestive system. The second patient's problems are behavioral and uniquely alien to Dr. Fulchuk. So now, every time Dr. Fulchuk meets a patient with these same symptoms, he wonders if the patient has a genuine disease of the digestive system or if the patient is psychiatric.

Dr. Ofri points out in *What Doctor's Feel* that physicians are more likely to come from wealthy families than the patients they treat. She also theorizes that physicians are more oriented to delayed gratification than the populations of patients they serve. Physicians, who not only earn bachelor's degrees, but also pro-actively seek an additional seven to 10 years of post-graduate education, are well versed in the concept of discipline. As a result of these biases, Dr. Ofri speculates that physicians, as a group, can have difficulty empathizing with their patients and can be repulsed by poor patient decisions, addicts, unhealthy lifestyle habits, and other behavioral health issues.

Dr. Ofri's comments appear to be confirmed by the research of Roter and Hall, cognitive researchers who have focused their studies specifically on physicians. Four studies comprising 250 physicians and 1,300 patients indicate that physicians tend to behave more negatively to their sicker and more emotionally distressed patients (e.g., those needing behavior health counseling) than they do to healthier patients.[86]

Empathy, by definition is a cognitive ability, while sympathy is an emotion with similar attributes. To measure physician empathy, researchers designed a survey of 20 questions called the Jefferson Empathy scale. The researchers found that the highest-scoring residents on the empathy scale tend to gravitate to primary care specialties, while those who score lowest tend to gravitate to surgery, anesthesiology, radiology, and other procedure-based specialties.

Physician empathy for health behaviors has serious implications for patients.

For example, an obese patient who has not been successful in self-administering a weight-loss regimen was viewed by his cardiologist and cardiac surgeon as a poor candidate for cardiac surgery because (1) he is too obese for surgery, and (2) he has not demonstrated the behaviors necessary for his self-care regimen after a major surgery. The behavioral ability to administer self-care is a factor in his physicians' treatment selection.

Similarly, when an elderly patient is non-compliant with a medication or therapy regimen, the patient's physician may consider whether dementia or depression are factors that are affecting the patient's cognitive abilities and the ability to take care of himself or herself.

Behavioral health and empathy are integral components of all disciplines of medicine and extremely critical in the war on chronic disease. Yet psychiatry, the focused study of behavioral health, has been devalued both subjectively and objectively by the rest of medicine and evidently insurers and employers.

To objectively compare the relative value that has been placed on psychiatry, we can review professional collections per work RVU (relative value unit). The work RVU is the universal unit of measure for comparing the relative amounts of value that are placed on various types of medical services. The American Medical Association convenes a multispecialty committee of physicians to periodically reassess the work RVU weights assigned to various medical services based on the complexity of the service, time, cost, and physician abilities. An evaluation and management office visit may be assessed one work RVU, while a colonoscopy procedure may be assessed 3.7 work RVUs.

The metric *professional collections per work RVU* is a good proxy for comparing how much money insurers and patients pay different types of physicians for a single unit of service. So if a family medicine physician collects $320,000 in a year and he or she performed services totaling 4,000 work RVUs, then this demonstrated $80 of professional collections per work RVU.

Of approximately 94 specialties referenced in the 2012 *MGMA Physician Compensation and Production Survey*, the physician specialty of psychiatry is ranked 92nd out of 94 at less than $50 of professional collections per work RVU at the median.[87] By comparison, for the same unit of service, one work RVU, radiologists are paid over $60, general surgeons are paid over $70, internists and family medicine physicians are paid over $75, orthopedic surgeons and pediatricians are paid over $85, ENT physicians are paid over $90, and dermatologists are paid over $100.

Clearly, when we control for the volume and types of services provided by various types of physicians by boiling all payments down to a single, work RVU comparison, the market for medical services values the physician discipline focusing on behavioral health near the very bottom.

Why in the world are psychiatrists the disdained stepchild of medicine when their focus on behavioral health is central to 75% of healthcare expenditures in the United States?

In medicine, the work RVU scale is used to determine the relative value of procedures performed by physicians. Unsurprisingly, surgical procedures like inpatient surgeries, deliveries, and Caesarean sections score very high on the work RVU scale. These are singular, acute procedures performed by specialists.

Replacing individual beliefs and biases with data gave the Oakland Athletics an advantage in professional baseball. After nearly 100 years, the market for baseball skills and talents was proved to still be very inefficient. The Oakland A's success proved this. In 2002, the Oakland A's payroll was $41 million compared to the New York Yankees' $125 million payroll. In the same year, Oakland and the Yankees both won 103 games. The Yankees paid over $1.2 million per win, while the A's paid $398,000 dollars per win.

Based on these statistics, you might infer that the owner of the New York Yankees, George Steinbrenner, got seriously ripped off, while the owners of the Oakland A's got a great deal that year. The Yankees paid just over three times as much money for every win as the Oakland A's.

Just as MLB teams invested too much money in fielding, health insurers and health systems have invested too much money in the wrong things.

Doctor Deals

If 75% of U.S. healthcare dollars are spent on largely preventable chronic diseases, why are the highest values placed on singular, acute surgical procedures? Why are successful medical treatments of heart disease, stroke, and diabetes valued so much lower than surgical procedures when it is the former that drives three-fourths of our healthcare costs? Shouldn't we place a higher value on successfully treating the diseases that account for the majority of our costs?

I am sorry to say that health insurers, including Medicare, grossly underprice the value of preventive medicine. As you can see in the following table, physician-led counseling for obesity, cardiovascular disease, diabetes, nutrition, depression, alcohol abuse, and STDs hovers between $18 and $26 for Medicare for about one-half of one work RVU of value. By comparison, work RVUs and payments are much higher for cardiac catheterizations at three to six work RVUs, gastric lap banding at 18, and Caesarean section surgery at 16. For Medicare, then, we can do some simple arithmetic to determine that a cardiac catheterization is worth six to 13 times as much as a behavior therapy session for cardiovascular disease, even though the latter can prevent the former. Similarly, the gastric lap banding procedure for CPT code 43770 is valued by Medicare at about 40 times the value placed on an obesity counseling session.

It is no wonder that surgical specialties are associated with so much prestige, while medical fields like psychiatry are sometimes shunned. The market values surgical care more, even though it is a relatively small piece of the overall cost of care. Just like MLB, the American healthcare market is inefficient.

HCPCS CODE	SHORT DESCRIPTION	NON-FACILITY PRICE
G0445	High inten beh couns STD 30m	$26.20
G0447	Behavior counsel obesity 15m	$25.52
G0443	Brief alcohol misuse counsel	$25.52
G0444	Depression screen annual	$18.37
G0446	Intens behave ther cardio dx	$25.52

William Osler, M.D., one of the founding professors at The Johns Hopkins Hospital, was quoted as saying, "It is much more important to know what sort of a patient has a disease than to know what kind of a disease a patient has."

A recent article in the American Heart Association's "Science News" boldly identified non-medical approaches to patient behavior change as the foundational factor for first-line defense against cardiovascular disease.[88] The authors were well versed in the psychological models of behavior change research and treatment adherence. They said:

> When it comes to reducing early deaths, medical care has a relatively minor role, potentially preventing 1 in 10 premature deaths. Rather, the single greatest opportunity to improve health and reduce premature death lies in favorably modifying unhealthy behaviors [...].

Naturally, among traditional medical professionals there are inherent inhibitions to dedicating serious time, analysis, and money to analyzing and modifying a patient's environmental factors.

According to the *2008 Health Tracking Physician Survey* of 4,720 physician members of the American Medical Association, 36% of primary care physicians and 27% of specialist physicians felt that not having adequate time with their patients during office visits was a major problem affecting their ability to provide quality care.[89] Incidentally, the same survey of physicians also reported that 43% of primary care physicians and 37% of specialist physicians identify patient non-compliance with treatment recommendation as a major problem area affecting their ability to provide quality care to patients.

It is unfortunate that some physicians do not have adequate time with their patients, because the quality of the baseline level of patient–physician communication is not very good to begin with. According to research, about half of patients leave their physician's office without a clear understanding of the advice or information received.[90,91] Health literacy is fundamental to treatment adherence. The whole Health Belief Model of patient adherence (see the section "Treatment Adherence") hinges on patients' having accurate perceptions about the severity of their diseases, the benefits of adhering to their treatment, and their expectations about their ability to succeed.

HEARTS & MINDS

In both medicine and military affairs, America has truly mastered its approach to the conventional search and destroy warfare. When a patient has a bacterial infection, antibiotic drugs are administered to wipe out the infection. When an MRI detects cancer, the tumor is surgically removed.

When you can see the enemy, you can easily destroy it. However, fighting chronic disease is more like fighting an insurgency war than a traditional search-and-destroy war—there is no tumor to remove or infectious disease to wipe out. In an insurgency war the enemy is everywhere, but you can't point at it. The enemy lives among the people and it is difficult to separate them. Fighting chronic disease is slow and messy.

Counterinsurgency warfare is actually an effort to win over the hearts and minds of the population, so *they* will help you fight the insurgents. Australian Lieutenant Colonel David Kilcullen's "Twenty-Eight Articles" paper on counterinsurgency has a great definition for insurgency that reverberates with some of the wisdom of treatment adherence science.[92]

Kilcullen defines insurgency as a competition with the insurgents for the right and the ability to win the hearts and minds of the population. He points out that military officers usually have more combat power than they should use in most situations, and that injudicious overuse of firepower has the unfortunate side effect of perpetuating the insurgency because it is harmful to the general public and creates bad public perceptions. To win an insurgency war, the public has to perceive that your actions benefit them and to trust your integrity and ability to fulfill your commitments to help them.

Until recently, there has been a prevalent disinclination among many army officers to engage in Military Operations Other Than War (MOOTW)—pronounced "Moot-wah." "Real men don't do MOOTW" is a common expression in the army. David Galula, one of the fathers of counterinsurgency, likened COIN activities to the same field as social work or pediatricians. Galula said COIN is eighty percent (80%) political action and only twenty percent (20%) military. Unfortunately, social work, pediatrics, and politics are not fields that many army officers would like to find themselves. After all, they became army officers to fight, not hold hands.

The same behaviors pervade the medical profession. In her book *God's Hotel*, Victoria Sweet shared a story about a physician who learned that one of his patients had been waiting to be discharged for several months after a stroke but was waiting for Medicaid to authorize payment on a pair of shoes for him to wear. The physician drove to Wal-Mart, bought a pair of shoes for the patient with his own money, and promptly discharged him from the hospital. In several months, it had not occurred to anyone to circumvent Medicaid and simply get the patient a pair of shoes without Medicaid's approval.

Colonel Kilcullen's wisdom resonates in the war on chronic disease because it is now evident, as discussed in the recent AHA article, that 90% of chronic disease preventive treatments are not medical in nature. In other words, medical doctors may not be the best professionals to treat 90% of the patients in the largest category of diseases.

TREATMENT ADHERENCE AND PATIENT BEHAVIOR THEORIES

When we dig deeper into the research, we find that there are several strong predictors for treatment adherence that are associated with individual patients' beliefs. The patient beliefs that are most strongly associated with treatment adherence are patient perceptions. These include perceived barriers to change, self-efficacy, perceived severity of the disease, perceived susceptibility to the disease, and perceived benefits to changing. [92,93,94,95] This research corroborates the contemporary Health Belief Model.

Health Belief Model

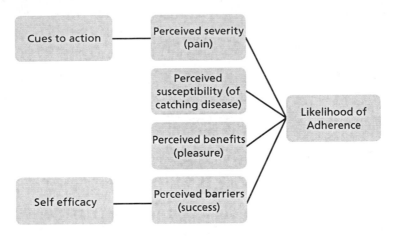

Research on social cognitive models, also called social learning theories, has also demonstrated that treatment adherence is dependent upon patients' perceptions, or beliefs, about the causative outcomes of their actions, their expectations of success, and environmental factors. These models integrate the idea that patients' expectations, or self-efficacy, will influence their attitudes, intentions, and behaviors.

Other models, including the theory of reasoned action and the theory of planned behavior, incorporate the former factors as well as a patient's intentions and subjective norms that influence patients. A patient's intentions, or desires, may be construed as the germ of all other actions, but they may be inhibited by a patient's perceptions about their control of their situation or their perceived ability to succeed.

Theory of Planned Behavior

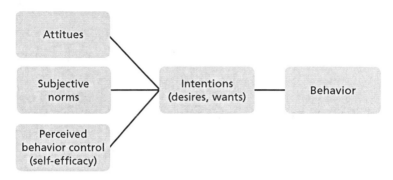

Therefore, in the context of chronic diseases, we have to make sure patients believe that they can successfully adhere to their treatment plans and that they want to succeed in adhering to their treatment plans.

Simply stating this seems dauntingly simple, but it is not. The questions that arise are:

1) How does one help a patient believe he or she can successfully accomplish adherence or a healthy outcome?

2) How does one make a patient want to accomplish that outcome?

Beliefs are a general feeling about something based on a person's internal inventory of information on that subject, including specific knowledge, experience, testimonials, and evidence for and against.

Some exciting research has been performed by Pro Change Behavior Systems in Rhode Island, a leader in the business of affecting health behavior changes in employers' workforces. Pro Change's founders are credited with developing the Transtheoretical Model of Behavior Change (TTM), which custom tailors interventions based on the readiness of the subjects

---

to change. Their scale of the readiness to change is the best known model for classifying chronic disease patients into archetypes for tailored treatments.

The TTM describes beliefs as being supported by internal lists of pros and cons. According to the TTM, at the early stages of behavior change, before a patient has made a conscious decision to engage or change a behavior, the efforts to modify this behavior mostly focus on creating more pros in favor of the behavior change that heavily outweigh the cons. In this sense, there is a sort of internal scale or compass within each individual that governs each of their behaviors. To change their behavior, they have to come to the realization that the pros of a particular behavior far outweigh the cons.

TREATMENT ADHERENCE EXPERTS[97]

I recently spoke with Robin DiMatteo, Ph.D., adherence expert and Distinguished Professor of Psychology at the University of California-Riverside. Dr. DiMatteo informed me that interest in the field of patient treatment adherence has recently exploded. During the past five years Dr. DiMatteo has been invited to lecture and train healthcare professionals on improving treatment adherence and enhancing provider–patient communication at over 60 major medical centers, including Harvard University, the Mayo Clinic, and the Cleveland Clinic, as well as accountable care organizations (ACOs), employer health coalitions, and health plans.

Medicare implemented the Hospital Readmission Reduction Program in 2013 as part of the Affordable Care Act (ACA) and it now reduces payments to hospitals with excess readmissions. This creates real financial incentives to keep chronic disease patients from being readmitted. Hospitals that did not meet the required metrics sustained a maximum payment penalty of 1.0% in 2013.

The, maximum penalty will increase to 3.0% by 2015. Heart attack and heart failure were targets in the program in 2013. Chronic obstructive pulmonary disease (COPD) will be added in 2015. Readmissions for heart attacks, heart failure, and COPD are affected by patient adherence to medications, attending cardiac or pulmonary rehabilitation, and lifestyle behaviors.

Additionally, there are now over 600 active ACOs in the United States. ACOs that minimize per member per month costs by reducing hospital readmissions and subsequent costs can receive up to 50% to 60% of the shared savings they generate. Chronic diseases comprise three-fourths of healthcare costs, so getting patients to adhere to their prescribed treatments is a key way to generate shared savings.

The U.S. Department of Health and Human Services (HHS) has afforded legal waivers to ACOs, including waivers to give patients incentives to adhere to their treatments. This means that ACOs and ACO providers may provide services or items to patients for free or below fair market value if four conditions are met:

1. The ACO has entered into a participation agreement and remains [active].

2. There is a reasonable connection between the items or services and the medical care of the beneficiary.

3. The items or services are in-kind (not money).

4. The items or services are preventive care items or services, or advance one or more of the following clinical goals:

    a. Adherence to treatment regime

    b. Adherence to drug regime

    c. Adherence to a follow-up care plan

d. Management of a chronic disease or condition

This patient incentive waiver enables ACO providers and participants to offer non-monetary incentives to patients with chronic diseases if the incentive is used to encourage treatment adherence. A few examples of in-kind services meeting this definition include (1) pharmacy delivery services, (2) patient transportation services to office visits and therapies, and (3) the provision of medication event monitoring systems (e.g., electronic medication caps) to patients.

According to the interim final rule, the intent of this patient incentive waiver is to "help ACOs foster patient engagement in improving quality, and lowering costs for Medicare and beneficiaries by removing any perceived obstacles created by the Beneficiary Inducements CMP or Federal anti-kickback statute."

While incentivizing patients is a simple solution to improving adherence, DiMatteo says incentives are not a sliver bullet solution.

"Even patients realize when they have adopted a behavior solely for the reward, not for an underlying, intrinsic goal," she says. "It's like a retail model. You can't get a customer to buy something by marking it down if they don't want it to begin with."

DiMatteo estimates that 275 million office visits per year are essentially wasted because patients either didn't understand the information they received or forgot it soon after.

"It is like going to Best Buy and throwing away 25% to 50% of what you buy when you leave the store," DiMatteo says.

Patients who do not understand what they are being told also tend not to ask questions. According to the 2003 federal National Assessment of Adult Literacy, only 12% of Americans were rated as having proficient health literacy, while about one-third were rated with basic or below basic health literacy.

Health systems can support their physician clinics by creating collateral materials and systems to develop and reinforce patient health literacy. After basic health literacy is established and patients understand what they are being told, patient beliefs are the second milestone for treatment adherence. As discussed in the health belief models, patients have to believe their illness is serious, that the treatment actually works, that the benefits of adhering to the treatment are greater than the costs, and that they have the ability to adhere to the treatment.

Patient belief barriers are demonstrated by commonplace 50% adherence rates for statins. Asymptomatic patients may not perceive the risks or cost–benefit analysis of adherence. Sophisticated adherence interventions and technologies are wasted if patient engagement is not attained first.

"A medication reminder system with wristwatch alarms is ineffective if patients don't *want* to take their pills," says DiMatteo. "They just turn off the alarm."

Identifying patient readiness for change has proven effective in custom-tailoring the most effective interventions to deploy. Patients at different stages of readiness will respond differently to different interventions. For example, a patient in the pre-contemplation or contemplation stage will likely not utilize a self-monitoring journal. For patients in this stage, general health literacy and treatment beliefs need to be addressed first.

Call Centers

Nurse call centers are a standard business model for care (case) management services offered by health plans as well as chronic disease management companies and health systems. DiMatteo believes telephonic interventions can be very effective as long as good signal reception is available.

Paul Cook, Ph.D., an associate professor and licensed psychologist at the University of Colorado, developed one such call center program called ScriptAssist Medication Adherence Programs. Cook trained nurses in the technique of motivational interviewing (MI), a style of patient interaction that focuses on eliciting information from patients rather than trying to educate them. Cook identifies MI as an appropriate approach for encouraging patient engagement.

"MI is good because it works with people who are not interested in changing a behavior as well as people who do not want to talk with you," Cook says. "It is good for building an initial alliance with patients."

As a consultant, Cook now trains pharmacists, physical therapists, respiratory therapists, physicians, medical assistants, dentists, and community health workers in MI techniques. He says even MI-trained pharmacists have demonstrated good success as contractors for call centers.

MI is a counseling style that has demonstrated effectiveness in over 70 clinical trials to promote behavior changes for substance abuse and non-addiction behaviors. MI has been described as a client-centered counseling style used for eliciting behavior change by enabling patients to explore and resolve ambivalence.[98,99] MI's creators called it:

> a way of being with people, that is also directive in seeking to move the person toward change by selectively evoking and strengthening the patient's own reasons for change.[100]

MI has three characteristics. These are collaboration, evocation, and autonomy.

1. MI is collaborative because the medical professional specifically does not assume a paternalistic, authoritarian role. The patient maintains his or her autonomy.

2. MI is evocative in that the medical professional can draw out perspectives and values from the patient instead of considering the patient's mind as an empty vessel that must be filled. The patient's internal values are elicited to evoke the changes. MI focuses on drawing behavior change forth from the patient, not pushing or pulling the patient to a stated objective.[100,101]

3. MI respects the patient's autonomy because the provider realizes that it is ultimately up to the patient to decide if he or she wants to change and how any changes would be accomplished.

Further, MI has four principles that are based on the three characteristics just described.

1. The provider is *empathetic* to the patient's perspective, without judging, criticizing, or blaming the patient for his or her thoughts, feelings, attitudes, motivations, or reasoning.

2. The goal of MI is to get patients to verbally *develop discrepancy* between their current behaviors and their values and goals on their own.[98,101] It is more powerful to have patients identify their reasons and motivations for change than to tell them why change is good.

3. The provider must *roll with resistance* and avoid confrontation and arguments. Arguing a point invokes defensiveness from the patient along with a decreased desire to adopt a behavior.

4. The provider must *support self-efficacy* and help patients improve their confidence in their ability to achieve success in their behavior modification.

MI is an important device in medical practice at a very basic practical level because studies have shown that patients (inpatients and outpatients) who receive MI are more likely to complete outpatient treatments, attend more outpatient sessions, and experience fewer re-hospitalizations than non-MI patients.[102]

In clinic settings, the average patient contact is 10 to 15 minutes.[103] This is a fundamental problem because motivational interviewing and similar behavioral health sessions can take 50 minutes at a time to complete.

Additionally, physicians who utilize an expert-driven practitioner-centered model may find it challenging to embrace the collaborative spirit of MI.[104] One of central facets of MI is to identify the patient as the expert in his or her own behaviors.

Clinic-Based Adherence Interventions

In a world where 15- to 20-minute office visits are the norm, primary care physicians may not have time to perform a thorough adherence assessment and face-to-face intervention with each patient. Cook says medical assistants, nurses, and physician extenders are ideal for training in MI and other techniques, and identifies this as a key way that health systems can support their primary care physicians.

"Nurses are well suited for MI training," says Cook. "I've also trained medical assistants and community health workers. Initially, there is sometimes a fixation on telling or talking at patients versus using open-ended questions and listening."

Cook says training typically involves a one- to two-day workshop and six to 12 months of supervised practice with occasional peer group meetings to discuss challenges and achievements.

Adopting patients as members of the care team is a cultural shift from the traditional paternalistic medical model. DiMatteo and Cook both agree that cultural, team acceptance of the collaborative approach is crucial to promoting treatment adherence in clinic settings. A good way to frame patients' role on the care team is to acknowledge that it is the patients who are self-managing their care the 99% of the time they are not present in the clinic.

Both DiMatteo and Cook emphasize the importance of non-judgmental, open-ended communication. The traditional medical interaction orients the medical provider as an authoritative or paternalistic figure. The terms *treatment adherence* and *non-adherence* have emerged, in part, because *patient compliance* and *non-compliance* carried negative connotations—portraying non-adherence as a direct failure of the patient and not a function of the environment or a gradual learning process. Treatment adherence research indicates that the use of fear and blame are counterproductive with patients who are not engaged. For patients who do not believe in the seriousness of their illness or efficacy of a prescribed treatment, their own self-enhancement biases can cause them to question and diminish negative feedback.

"'Can you tell me how you have been taking your medicine?'" says DiMatteo, "is better than 'Have you been taking your medication?' or 'Did you take your medication yesterday?'."

"I often start by just asking the patient what they think they will do," says Cook, "Or ask them to rate their readiness on a one-to-10 scale."

CLOSING REMARKS

Kyle and I have had the great fortune to work in a complex and challenging industry that regularly presents opportunities to exercise our creativity. I am continually impressed by the high caliber physicians, attorneys, and health executives with whom we continually have the pleasure to work. Without being constantly pushed by such demanding clients and high standards of medical excellence, we would not have been able to develop this book.

I love working on deals that focus on improving medical outcomes. There are great opportunities for deals in primary care and post-acute medicine to make real improvements in the treatment of cardiovascular disease, diabetes, COPD, and cancer. These are what I love to do. I love deals that *prevent* hospital admissions.

If this message resonates with you, please don't waste any of your time on bad doctor deals. We can figure out a way to do better deals every time.

Nicholas Newsad, MHSA

Healthcare Transaction Advisors, LLC

Endnotes

1 American Health Lawyers Association. Accessed March 2014. "Corporate Practice of Medicine." http://www.healthlawyers. org/hlresources/Health%20Law%20Wiki/Corporate%20 Practice%20of%20Medicine.aspx.

2 Liaison Committee on Medical Education. http://www.lcme.org/directory.htm. Accessed March 2014. "Medical School Directory."

3 U.S. Department of Health and Human Services. Accessed March 2014. "The Physician Workforce: Projections and Research into Current Issues Affecting Supply and Demand. December 2008." http://bhpr.hrsa.gov/healthworkforce/reports/physwfissues.pdf.

4 Association of American Medical Colleges. Accessed March 2014. "2011 State Physician Workforce Data Book." https://www.aamc.org/download/263512/data/statedata2011.pdf.

5 American Hospital Association. Accessed March 2014. "Fast Facts on US Hospitals." http://www.aha.org/research/rc/stat-studies/ fast-facts.shtml.

6 Association of American Medical Colleges. Accessed March 2014. "About the AAMC." https://www.aamc.org/about/.

7 Arnedt JT, Owens J, Crouch M, Stahl J, Carskadon MA. . "Neurobehavioral Performance of Residents After Heavy Night Call vs After Alcohol Ingestion." *JAMA*. 2005;294(9):1025-1033.

8 American Health Lawyers Association. "Stark: Overview of Issue." Accessed April 2014. http://www.healthlawyers.org/hlresources/Health%20Law%20 Wiki/Stark.aspx.

9   December 31, 2013 10-K.

10   December 31, 2013 10-K.

11   Becker's Healthcare. Accessed March 2014. "HCA Outpatient
     Volumes Increase in First Quarter of 2012."
     http://www.beckersasc.com/asc-transactions-and-valuation-
     issues/hca-outpatient-volumes-increase-in-first-quarter-of-2012.
     html

12   Cheryl Proval. "Imaging-center Growth Hits the Wall in 2013;
     Volumes Plummeted in 2011." Accessed April. 2014. *Radiology
     Business Journal.*
     http://www.radiologybusiness.com/topics/business/imaging-
     center-growth-hits-wall-2013-volumes-plummeted-2011.

13   Greg Farrell. Accessed March 2014. "Scrushy acquitted of all 36
     charges." *USA TODAY.*
     http://usatoday30.usatoday.com/money/industries/health/2005-
     06-28-scrushy_x.htm.

14   Kyle Whitmire. "Ex-Governor and Executive Convicted of
     Bribery." Accessed March 2014.
     http://www.nytimes.com/2006/06/30/us/30verdict.html?_r=0.

15   42 U.S.C. § 1320a-7b

16   American Health Lawyers Association. "Federal Anti-Kickback
     Statute Primer." Accessed April 8, 2014. http://publish.
     healthlawyers.org/Events/Programs/Materials/Documents/
     FC12/101_homchick_williams.pdf.

17   State Medical Board of Ohio. "Statement of the State Medical
     Board of Ohio .on the Corporate Practice of Medicine." http://

med.ohio.gov/pdf/Corporate%20Practice%20of%20Medicine%20
Statement.pdf.

18 Centers for Medicare & Medicaid Services. "Decision Memo for
    Cardiac Catheterization Performed In Other Than A Hospital
    Setting (CAG-00166N)." Accessed March 2014.
    http://www.cms.gov/medicare-coverage-database/details/
    nca-decision-memo.aspx?NCAId=15&ver=16&NcaName
    =Cardiac+Catheterization+Performed+In+Other+Than+A+
    Hospital+Setting&bc= BEAAAAAAEAAA&&fromdb=true.

19 HCA Website. "Our History." Accessed April 2014. http://
    hcahealthcare.com/about/our-history.dot.

20 Anne Pettinger. "Jim Alderson: A Whistleblower's Odyssey."
    Accessed April 2014.
    http://www.montana.edu/mountainsandminds/article.
    php?article=9280.

21 Scott Hiaasen and John Dorschner. "Rick Scott touts CEO
    experience in run for Florida governor, to a degree." Accessed
    April 2014. *Tampa Bay Times*, http://www.tampabay.com/news/
    politics/rick-scott-touts-ceo-experience-in-run-for-florida-
    governor-to-a-degree/1105385.

22 Kurt Eichenwald. "HCA to Pay $95 Million In Fraud Case."
    Accessed April 2014. *The New York Times*. http://www.nytimes.
    com/2000/12/15/business/hca-to-pay-95-million-in-fraud-case.
    html.

23 Kurt Eichenwald. "U.S. Expands Search of Columbia/HCA
    in Texas." Accessed April 2014. *The New York Times*. http://
    partners.nytimes.com/library/financial/032197columbia-hca-
    investigate.html.

24 Department of Justice. HCA - The Health Care Company &
    Subsidiaries To Pay $840 Million In Criminal Fines and Civil
    Damages And Penalties: Largest Government Fraud Settlement in
    U.S. History." Accessed April 2014.
    http://www.justice.gov/opa/pr/2000/December/696civcrm.htm.

25 Kurt Eichenwald. : 2 Leaders Are Out At Health Giant As Inquiry
    Goes On ." Accessed April 2014. *The New York Times.*
    http://www.nytimes.com/1997/07/26/business/2-leaders-are-
    out-at-health-giant-as-inquiry-goes-on.html.

26 Daniels Fund Ethics Initiative-University of New Mexico.
    "Hospital Corporation of America: Learning from Past
    Mistakes?." Accessed April 2014. http://danielsethics.mgt.unm.
    edu/pdf/HCA.pdf.

27 Tristram Korten. "Rick Scott profits off the uninsured." Accessed
    April 2014. *Salon.* http://www.salon.com/2009/09/30/rick_scott_
    one/.

28 John Schilling. *Undercover: How I Went from Company Man to FBI
    Spy and Exposed the Worst Healthcare Fraud in U.S. History.* Page
    232. AMACON: New York, NY. 2008.

29 Corporate Integrity Agreement Between the Office of the
    Inspector General of the United States Department of Health and
    Human Services and HCA-The Healthcare Company. Accessed
    April 2014. http://oig.hhs.gov/fraud/cia/agreements/the_hc_
    co_121400.pdf.

30 Department of Justice. "Largest Health Care Fraud Case In U.S.
    History Settled HCA Investigation Nets Record Total Of $1.7
    Billion." Accessed April 2014.
    http://www.justice.gov/opa/pr/2003/June/03_civ_386.htm.

31 HCA Website. About Our Company. Accessed April 2014. http://
    hcahealthcare.com/about/.

32 David R. Olmos. "National Medical-SEC Settlement OKd
    : Health care: The hospital company had agreed to pay $379
    million in connection with fraud charges." Accessed April 2014.
    The Los Angeles Times. http://articles.latimes.com/1994-07-13/
    business/fi-15135_1_fraud-charges.

33 Kurt Eichenwald. "OPERATING PROFITS: Mining Medicare;
    How One Hospital Benefited From Questionable Surgery."
    Accessed April 2014. *The New York Times.*
    http://www.nytimes.com/2003/08/12/business/operating-
    profits-mining-medicare-one-hospital-benefited-questionable-
    surgery.html.

34 Kurt Eichenwald. "Tenet Healthcare Paying $54 Million In Fraud
    Settlement." Accessed April 2014. *The New York Times.*
    http://www.nytimes.com/2003/08/07/business/tenet-healthcare-
    paying-54-million-in-fraud-settlement.html.

35 Lisa Girion. "U.S. Settles With Tenet, Doctors on Surgeries."
    Accessed April 2014. *The Los Angeles Times.*
    http://articles.latimes.com/2005/nov/16/business/fi-tenet16.

36 Uncredited. "Tenet Hospital Administrator Is Arrested in Federal
    Inquiry." Accessed April 2014. *The New York Times.*
    http://www.nytimes.com/2003/09/25/business/tenet-hospital-
    administrator-is-arrested-in-federal-inquiry.html.

37 Press release. "Tenet Receives OIG Civil Subpoena for
    Information Regarding Agreements With Physician Group."
    Accessed April 2014. *Business Wire.*
    http://www.businesswire.com/news/home/20030417005683/en/
    Tenet-Receives-OIG-Civil-Subpoena-Information-Agreements.

38 Debora Vrana. "U.S. Probe at a Tenet Hospital Expands."
    Accessed April 2014. *The Los Angeles Times.*
    http://articles.latimes.com/2003/jul/16/business/fi-tenet16.

39 Uncredited. "Tenet Healthcare Says It Faces Florida Medicaid
    Investigation." Accessed April 2014. *The New York Times.* http://
    www.nytimes.com/2003/08/09/business/tenet-healthcare-says-
    it-faces-florida-medicaid-investigation.html.

40 Lisa Girion. "New Data Sought in Federal Probe of
    Tenet."Accessed April 2014. *The Los Angeles Times.*
    http://articles.latimes.com/2004/mar/04/business/fi-subpoena4.

41 Melissa Davis. "Tenet Doctor Probe Widens." Accessed April
    2014. *TheStreet.com.* http://www.thestreet.com/story/10187370/1/
    tenet-doctor-probe-widens.html.

42 Katherine Vogt. "Tenet settles case on referral kickbacks"
    Accessed April 2013. *American Medical News.* http://www.
    amednews.com/article/20060605/business/306059991/7/.

43 Department of Justice Press Release. "Tenet Healthcare
    Corporation to Pay U.S. more than $900 Million to Resolve False
    Claims Act Allegations." Accessed April 2014. http://www.justice.
    org/opa/pr/2006/june/06_civ_406.html.

44 Cornell University Law School. 42 CFR § 489.20(r)(2) and 42
    CFR § 489.24(j). Accessed March 2014. http://www.law.cornell.
    edu/cfr/text/42/489.20 and http://www.gpo.gov/fdsys/pkg/CFR-
    2010-title42-vol5/pdf/CFR-2010-title42-vol5-sec489-24.pdf.

45 California Children's Services. "Chapter 3 – Provider Standards,
    Standards for Pediatric Intensive Care Units." Accessed March 2014.
    http://www.dhcs.ca.gov/services/ccs/Documents/PICU.pdf.

46 Tom Kisken. "Doctors think of suicide more, survey shows."
    Ventura County Star. Accessed March 2014. http://www.vcstar.
    com/news/2011/jan/22/medical-casualties-doctors-think-of-
    suicide-more/?print=1.

47 American Health Lawyers Association. Accessed April 2014.
    "Gainsharing." http://www.healthlawyers.org/hlresources/
    Health%20Law%20Wiki/Gainsharing.aspx.

48 National Public Radio. Accessed March 2014. "Could Kaiser
    Permanente's Low-Cost Health Care Be Even Cheaper?" http://
    www.npr.org/blogs/health/2012/06/26/155726049/could-kaiser-
    permanentes-low-cost-health-care-be-even-cheaper.

49 California Department of Managed Health Care. Accessed March
    2014. "Health Plan Financial Summary Report." http://wpso.
    dmhc.ca.gov/flash/.

50 http://www.colorado.gov/cs Complete 2011 Statistical Report

51 Wiki Commons. Accessed April 2014.
    http://upload.wikimedia.org/wikipedia/commons/thumb/e/ee/
    Frequency_reuse.svg/400px-Frequency_reuse.svg.png.

52 Federal Trade Commission. Accessed March 2014. "FTC
    Challenges Carilions Acquisition of Outpatient Medical Clinics."
    http://www.ftc.gov/opa/2009/07/carilion.shtm.

53 Federal Trade Commission. Accessed March 2014. "Commission
    Order Restores Competition Eliminated by Carilion Clinics
    Acquisition of Two Outpatient Clinics." http://www.ftc.gov/
    opa/2009/10/carilion.shtm.

54 Federal Trade Commission. Accessed March 2014. "Phoebe

Putney Health System, Inc., Phoebe Putney Memorial Hospital, Inc., Phoebe North, Inc., HCA Inc., Palmyra Park Hospital, Inc., and Hospital Authority of Albany-Dougherty County, In the Matter of." http://www.ftc.gov/os/adjpro/d9348/130222ccmoliftstay.pdf.

55 Federal Trade Commission. Accessed April 2014. "Hospital Authority and Phoebe Putney Health System Settle FTC Charges That Acquisition of Palmyra Park Hospital Violated U.S. Antitrust Laws." http://www.ftc.gov/news-events/press-releases/2013/08/hospital-authority-and-phoebe-putney-health-system-settle-ftc.

56 Federal Trade Commission. Accessed March 2014. "Citing Likely Anticompetitive Effects, FTC Requires ProMedica Health System to Divest St. Luke's Hospital in Toledo, Ohio, Area." http://www.ftc.gov/opa/2012/03/promedica.shtm.

57 Federal Trade Commission. Accessed March 2014. "OSF Healthcare System Abandons Plan to Buy Rockford in Light of FTC Lawsuit; FTC Dismisses its Complaint Seeking to Block the Transaction." http://www.ftc.gov/opa/2012/04/rockford2.shtm.

58 Federal Trade Commission. Accessed March 2014. "FTC Order Will Restore Competition for Adult Cardiology Services in Reno, Nevada." http://www.ftc.gov/opa/2012/08/renownhealth.shtm.

59 Federal Trade Commission. Accessed March 2014. "FTC and Pennsylvania Attorney General Challenge Reading Health Systems Proposed Acquisition of Surgical Institute of Reading." http://www.ftc.gov/opa/2012/11/reading.shtm.

60 Federal Trade Commission. Accessed March 2014. "FTC and Idaho Attorney General Challenge St. Luke's Health System's Acquisition of Saltzer Medical Group as Anticompetitive." http://

www.ftc.gov/opa/2013/03/stluke.shtm.

61 Becker's Hospital Review. Accessed March 2014. "25 Largest
   Non-Profit Hospital Systems - July 24, 2012." http://www.
   beckershospitalreview.com/lists/25-largest-non-profit-hospital-
   systems.html.

62 Gregg Blesch. "Christ Hospital, Health Alliance OK
   separation terms." Accessed April 2014. *Modern Healthcare.*
   http://www.modernhealthcare.com/article/20090119/
   MAGAZINE/901169955.

63 Robert Wood Johnson Foundation. Accessed March 2014.
   "Chronic Care: Making the Case for Ongoing Care."
   http://www.rwjf.org/en/research-publications/find-rwjf-
   research/2010/01/chronic-care.html.

64 Centers for Disease Control and Prevention. Accessed March
   2014. "Chronic Disease Prevention and Health Promotion."
   http://www.cdc.gov/chronicdisease/index.htm.

65 Care Continuum Alliance. Accessed March 2014. "Table
   J4 – Financial Measures." *Implementation and Evaluation: A
   Population Health Guide for Primary Care Models.* 2012. http://
   selfmanagementalliance.org/wp-content/uploads/2013/11/A-
   Population-Health-Guide-for-Primary-Care-Models-
   CareContinAlliance.pdf.

66 Goldberg RJ, Ciampa J, Lessard D, Meyer TE, Spencer FA Long-
   term Survival After Heart Failure: A Contemporary Population-
   Based Perspective. *Arch Intern Med.* 2007;167(5):490–496.

67 Ho KK, Anderson KM, Kannel WB, Grossman W, Levy D.
   Survival after the onset of congestive heart failure in Framingham
   Heart Study subjects. *Circulation.* 1993 Jul;88(1):107–15.

68 Smart N, Marwick TH. Exercise training for patients with heart failure: a systematic review of factors that improve mortality and morbidity. *Am J Med.* 2004 May 15;116(10):693–706.

69 Suaya JA, Shepard DS, Morman SL, Ades PA, Prottas J. Stason WB. Use of cardiac rehabilitation by Medicare beneficiaries after myocardial infarction or coronary bypass surgery. *Circulation.* 2007; 116(15):1653–1662.

70 Daly J, Sindone AP, Thompson DR, Hancock K, Chang E, Davidson P. Barriers to participation in and adherence to cardiac rehabilitation programs: a critical literature review. *Prog Cardiovasc Nurs.* 2002; 17(1):8–17.

71 Centers for Medicare & Medicaid Services. Accessed March 2014. "Proposed Decision Memo for Cardiac Rehabilitation (CR) Programs - Chronic Heart Failure." http://www.cms.gov/medicare-coverage-database/details/nca-proposed-decision-memo.aspx?NCAId=270.

72 Peikes D, Chen A, Schore J, Brown R. Accessed March 2014. "Effects of Care Coordination on Hospitalization, Quality of Care, and Health Care Expenditures Among Medicare Beneficiaries--15 Randomized Trials." February 11, 2009, Vol. 301, No. 6. http://jama.jamanetwork.com/article.aspx?articleid=183370.

73 Klein, Ezra. If this were a pill, you'd do anything to get it. 4.28.2013. Washington Post Blog. http://www.washingtonpost.com/blogs/wonkblog/wp/2013/04/28/if-this-was-a-pill-youd-do-anything-to-get-it/

74 Josh Pennell. "Local approach to COPD discussed at chronic disease conference." Accessed March 2014. *The Telegram.*

http://www.thetelegram.com/News/Local/2013-11-08/
article-3471498/Local-approach-to-COPD-discussed-at-chronic-
disease-conference/1.

75 Agency for Healthcare Research and Quality. Accessed March
    2014. "Medical Center Establishes Infrastructure to Manage Care
    Under Capitated Contracts, Leading to Better Chronic Care
    Management and Lower Utilization and Costs." http://www.
    innovations.ahrq.gov/content.aspx?id=3651.

76 Health Affairs Blog. Accessed March 2014. "Broadening the
    ACA Story: A Totally Accountable Care Organization." http://
    healthaffairs.org/blog/2014/01/23/broadening-the-aca-story-a-
    totally-accountable-care-organization/.

77 Cramer JA, Benedict A, Muszbek N, Keskinasian A, Khan ZM.
    The significance of compliance and persistence in the treatment
    of diabetes, hypertension and dyslipidaemia: a review. *Int J Clin
    Pract*. 2008 January; 62(1):76–87.

78 New England Healthcare Institute. Accessed April 2014,
    "Thinking Outside the Pillbox: A System-wide Approach to
    Improving Patient
    Medication Adherence for Chronic Disease." 2009.
    http://adhereforhealth.org/wp-content/uploads/pdf/
    ThinkingOutsidethePillbox_Report.pdf

79 Agency for Healthcare Research and Quality. Accessed April
    2014, "Closing the Quality Gap Series: Medication Adherence
    Interventions: Comparative Effectiveness." September 11, 2012.
    http://effectivehealthcare.ahrq.gov/index.cfm/search-for-guides-
    reviews-and-reports/?pageaction=displayproduct&product
    id=1249

80 McKenney JM, Munroe WP, Wright JT Jr. Impact of an

electronic medication compliance aid on long-term blood pressure control. *J Clin Pharmacol*. 1992 Mar;32(3):277–83.

81 Demonceau J, Ruppar T, Kristanto P, Hughes DA, Fargher E, Kardas P, De Geest S, Dobbels F, Lewek P, Urquhart J, Vrijens B; ABC project team. AARDEX Group Ltd. Identification and assessment of adherence-enhancing interventions in studies assessing medication adherence through electronically compiled drug dosing histories: a systematic literature review and meta-analysis. *Drugs*. 2013 May;73(6):545–62.

82 Epstein LH & Cluss PA. A behavioral medicine perspective on adherence to long-term medical regimens. *J Consult Clin Psychol*. 1982;50:950–971.

83 Brownell KD & Cohen LR. Adherence to dietary regimens: 1. An overview of research. *Behav Med* 1995;20:149–154.

84 Wilfley D & Brownell KD. Physical activity and diet in weight loss. In: Dishman RK, ed. Advances in exercise adherence. Champaign, IL: Human Kinetics 1994:361–393.

85 Norman P, Abraham C, Conner M, eds. Understanding and changing health behaviour: From health beliefs to self-regulation. Amsterdam: Harwood, 2000.

86 Hall JA, Roter DL, Milburn MA, Daltroy LH. Patients' health as a predictor of physician and patient behavior in medical visits. A synthesis of four studies. *Med Care*. 1996 Dec; 34(12):1205–18.

87 Medical Group Management Association. Table 23.1 Physician Collections to Physician Work RVUs Ratio (CMS RBRVS

Method)(NPP Excluded) All Physicians. 2012 *MGMA Physician Compensation and Production Survey.*

88   Barry A. Franklin, PhD; Jenna Brinks, MS; Harold Friedman, MD. Accessed April 2014. "Foundational Factors for Cardiovascular Disease: Behavior Change as a First-Line Preventive Strategy." http://my.americanheart.org/professional/ScienceNews/Foundational-Factors-for-Cardiovascular-Disease-Behavior-Change-as-a-First-Line_UCM_457215_Article.jsp.

89   Deshpande SP & DeMello J. A comparative analysis of factors that hinder primary care physicians' and specialist physicians' ability to provide high-quality care. *Health Care Manag* (Frederick). 2011 Apr-Jun;30(2):172–8.

90   Crane JA. Patient comprehension of doctor-patient communication on discharge from the emergency department. *J Emerg Med.* 1997 Jan-Feb:1 5(1):1–7.

91   Roter DL & Hall JA. Studies of doctor-patient interaction. *Annu Rev Public Health.* 1989:10:163–80.

92   Kilcullen, David. Accessed April 2014, "Twenty-Eight Articles: Fundamentals of Company-Level Counterinsurgency." *IOSPHERE, Joint Information Operations Center.* http://www.au.af.mil/info-ops/iosphere/iosphere_summer06_kilcullen.pdf.

93   Janz NK & Becker MH. The Health Belief Model: a decade later. *Health Educ Behav.* 1984 January 1, 1984; 11(1):1–47.

94   Wallace LS. Osteoperosis prevention in college women: application of the expanded Health Belief Model. *AM J Health Behav.* 2002 May-Jun;26(3):163–72.

95   Aljasem LI, Peyrot M, Wissow L, Rubin RR. The impact of

barriers and self-efficacy on self-care behaviors in type 2 diabetes. *Diabetes Educ.* 2001 May-Jun;27(3):393–404.

96   Lee SK, Kan B-Y, Kim H-G, Son Y-J. Predictors of Medication Adherence in Elderly Patients with Chronic Diseases Using Support Vector Models. *Healthc Inform Res.* 2013 March; 19(1): 33–41.

97   Nicholas Newsad. "Providers Zeroing in On Patient Behavior." Accessed April 2014. *Healthcare Finance News,* http://www.healthcarefinancenews.com/news/providers-zeroing-patient-behavior.

98   Miller WR & Rollnick S. (1991). *Motivational interviewing: Preparing people to change addictive behaviors.* New York: Guilford Press.

99   Rollnick S & Miller WR. (1995). What is motivational interviewing? *Behavioral and Cognitive Psychotherapy,* 23, 325–334.

100 Miller WR. (2004). Motivational interviewing in service to health promotion. The art of health promotion: Practical information to make programs more effective. *American Journal of Health Promotion,* 18(3), 1–10.

101 Miller WR & Rollnick S. (2002). *Motivational interviewing: Preparing people for change* (2nd ed.). New York: Guilford Press.

102 Daley DC, Salloum IM, Zuckoff A, Kirisci L, Thase ME. (1998). Increasing treatment adherence among outpatients with depression and cocaine dependence: Results of a pilot study. *American Journal of Psychiatry,* 155(11), 1611–1613.

103 Emmons KM & Rollnick S. (2001) Motivational interviewing in health care settings: Opportunities and limitations. *American*

Journal of Preventive Medicine, 20(1), 68–74.

104 Resnicow K, Dilorio C, Soet JE, Borrelli B, Hecht J, Ernst D. (2002). Motivational interviewing in health promotion: It sounds like something is changing. *Health Psychology,* 21(5), 444–451.